Family, Household, and the Life-course;
Studies in British Society

Edited
by
Alan Warde and Nicholas Abercrombie

Framework Press Educational Publishers Ltd.
Parkfield
Greaves Road
LANCASTER
LA1 4TZ

First published 1994

ISBN 1 85008 064 X

**Family, Household, and the Life-course;
Studies in British Society**

A catalogue record for the pack is available from the British Library

Typeset by Blackpool Typesetting Services Ltd., Blackpool

Printed at Alden Press Limited,
Oxford and Northampton, Great Britain

Cover Design by John Angus

Family, Household, and the Life-course;
Studies in British Society

Table of Contents

Notes on Contributors

Nicholas Abercrombie – Professor of Sociology, University of Lancaster

Alistair Billam – Postgraduate Research Student, Sociology Department, University of Lancaster

Janet Finch – Professor of Social Relations and Pro-Vice-Chancellor, University of Lancaster

Pauline Hare – Postgraduate Research Student, Sociology Department, University of Lancaster

Wendy Langford – Postgraduate Research Student, Sociology Department, University of Lancaster

Stephanie Lawler – Postgraduate Research Student, Sociology Department, University of Lancaster

Sandie Lawrinson – Lecturer in Sociology in the School of Social Sciences, Staffordshire University

Celia Lury – Lecturer in Sociology, University of Lancaster

David Morgan – Senior Lecturer in Sociology, University of Manchester

Sue Penna – Lecturer in Applied Social Science, University of Lancaster

Andrew Sayer – Lecturer in Sociology, University of Lancaster

Roger Walters – Postgraduate Research Student, Sociology Department, University of Lancaster

Alan Warde – Reader in Sociology, University of Lancaster

Anne Witz – Lecturer in Social Policy, University of Birmingham

Introduction

The principal aim of this book is to describe some important recent empirical, sociological studies of households. Each chapter is written to a rough formula, placing an empirical study in its intellectual and historical context, describing the methods used in the investigation, summarising key findings, and giving a brief résumé of critical evaluations of the work. Each provides valuable information about sociological methods and the most recent research findings on key themes in the sociology of families and the life-course in Britain.

Readers might use the chapters to discover what is in a particular recent study; to obtain an overview of recent empirical research in the general area of the sociology of households; to consider a series of examples of the way that evidence is linked to social scientific conclusions; and to evaluate different methods of data collection and analysis.

Each chapter has three objectives:

1 – to introduce new empirical material on important topics not yet available in popular textbooks;

2 – to reproduce materials – tables, verbatim passages from interviews, etc., appearing in the chapters and their appendices – which will help the reader appreciate the character of the evidence used to support the book's conclusions;

3 – to give as an impartial an evaluation as possible of the studies under review. Our authors have consulted the full range of published reflection on the books discussed, often using book reviews in the major sociological journals. In cases where there has been little published commentary, usually where the studies are very recent, authors offer their own critical judgments. However, throughout, the aim has been to offer a 'plain' account, trying to avoid prejudging for the reader the strengths and the limitations of each study.

The reason for pursuing this third objective is that we hope the book will be used by students as a device for learning and practising the exercise of critical judgment about sociological research. Consequently, each chapter stands alone and there has been no attempt to construct an integrated account of the institutions examined. We anticipate that chapters will be read separately and not necessarily in the order printed. This is a resource book rather than a textbook. Nevertheless, taken together, two important, integrating themes, one substantive, the other methodological, can be traced through the chapters.

First, much knowledge can be gained into the current state of domestic life in Britain, a topic of immense personal and political/ public concern. In recent years, sociologists have tended to insist that the most appropriate analytic focus is the household, because the status of kinship and marriage has become more uncertain as a consequence of continuous rapid social change. Many chapters refer to studies of aspects of the transformation of family and marriage, ones which describe and qualify popular impressions about the fragmentation of family life. They demonstrate the high expectations of marriage held by those getting wed, as well as pathologies of the marital condition such as domestic violence, adultery and divorce. The obligations associated with kinship are shown to be still extensive, but variable in the degree to which they are binding. Indeed, the extent of the variation in the patterns and organization of domestic life is one of the most startling general impressions. Paradoxically, the evidence implies that people's values and expectations are much more uniform than their behaviour with respect to marital and kinship relations.

The concept of 'life-course' has superseded that of 'life-cycle' among sociologists partly also because of the fragmentation of patterns of domestic life. Life-cycle suggests a regularity and uniformity of experience, a passage through successive stages of domestic organization in a predictable order. However, child-bearing outside marriage, divorcees beginning second families, the public emergence of alternatives to heterosexuality, changing definitions of women's social role, even simply the tendency for people to live longer, have disrupted previously established patterns. Now, a stage in the life-course, for example bringing up young children, which imposes a set of powerful constraints on social behaviour, no longer occurs predominantly among young, newly married couples. The concept of life-course is, thus, helpful in separating analytically domestic circumstances from the process of ageing. It still allows sociologists to analyse in detail particular stages of household development and some of the chapters deal precisely with the learning processes of young children, the nature of the transition to adulthood, and routine domestic activities like housework and watching television. These practices vary between social groups and are subject to degrees of change.

Reading all the chapters for their substantive content thus gives extensive, detailed and authoritative insight into the nature of contemporary British households. The studies examined, however, use many different methods of collecting information from which to draw their conclusions. Surveys, in-depth interviews with individuals, group discussions, observation, ethnographies, comparison of cases, and the secondary analysis of data, are all represented. Most of the currently accepted methods of data collection, each implying somewhat different forms of research design and analysis, can be considered and compared in the context of the sociology of households. Their differences, and their typical strengths and limitations, can be appreciated as they work themselves through real studies. We provide real examples of studies based on different methods, to make apparent how different methodologies (a topic so often discussed in a dry, technical and abstract fashion) generate different kinds of data and authorise different kinds of conclusion. Indeed, there is some sense in which alternative methods seem to provide contradictory conclusions. However, the range, merits and consequences of alternatives approaches to systematic and rigorous social research can be appreciated in a lively and grounded fashion through the fifteen studies reviewed in the chapters of this book.

Alan Warde and Nick Abercrombie
Lancaster, December 1993

1

The Early Years of Marriage

Penny Mansfield and Jean Collard (1988), *The Beginning of the Rest of Your Life?*, Basingstoke, Macmillan.

David Morgan

Marriage: A Public Issue and a Private Concern

Marital problems are rarely out of today's headlines. The marriages of members of the British Royal Family or of Cabinet Ministers frequently feature in our tabloid press and there are regular discussions of Britain's divorce rate, currently one of the highest in Europe. Discussions on topics such as 'Is Marriage Outmoded?' are popular topics for newspaper articles and television programmes.

In such a context, it is natural for those individuals who are embarking upon marriage for the first time to express concern about their relationships, their 'normality' and the likelihood of their lasting. Couples are increasingly, it seems, seeking to understand the relationships between their own particular marriage and 'marriages in general' (Mansfield and Collard, 1988, p.5).

Such couples will find no shortage of advice. From statistical information they will learn that people are getting married later in life than was the case for earlier generations and that cohabitation is becoming increasingly common, especially among the younger age groups (see *Tables 1.1, 1.2*, pp.12, 13). They will learn that there is a likelihood that one in three or more marriages will end in divorce and that an increasing proportion of marriages include at least one formerly-married person. Yet with all this public comment there is still relatively little research on the everyday experiences of, and feelings about, marriage.

The Beginning of the Rest of Your Life? attempts to repair this omission. It focusses upon the processes of becoming a married couple and then goes on to explore the early years of marriage. These explorations include the living arrangements; how the couples

decided upon the appropriate division of labour within the home and
how they achieved some kind of balance between paid employment and
domestic life, and how they responded to conflicts and differences of
opinion within marriage. Running through all these accounts is an
attempt to grasp how the partners themselves viewed marriage and
their hopes and fears for the future.

In theoretical terms, the authors broadly located themselves within
the tradition of 'interactionism'. They were less concerned with an
analysis of how marriage as an institution functioned, or failed to function, in relation to the wider society and more concerned with questions
of 'how?': how people got married, how they reached decisions within
the home, and so on. This implies a focus on process:

> Above all we required an approach in which flux, uncertainty and
> change would be regarded as central to the understanding of human
> behaviour. (Mansfield and Collard, 1988, p.30)

Research Design

Mansfield and Collard decided to concentrate on first-time marriages
so as to exclude some of the different issues that might arise where one
or both of the partners were entering into a second marriage. Their
couples came from the London area and were reached through contacts
with local churches. They were unable to gain permission to use registry offices but this was perhaps less of a problem than might be
imagined since two out of every three first-time marriages are
celebrated in church. They interviewed 65 couples under the age of
thirty, three months after the wedding ceremony. A follow-up study
was part of the programme and these interviews were to take place
after five years of marriage. This second stage of the research is now
complete and a second volume is expected. The main research instru-
ment was the interview, described by the authors as 'a conversation
with a purpose' (ibid., p.40). The object was to develop a research tool
that was close to a natural conversation and where, while aiming to
cover a certain number of topics, the order and the way in which these
topics were covered depended to a large extent upon the process of the
'conversation' as it went along. The aim was to develop a flexible and
open interview, one which would try to avoid producing routine or
stereotypical responses and which could get close to the reality, was
well as to the ideal, of marriage.

It was decided that the all-women research team should interview
both partners separately, but at the same time, yielding a total of 130,
two to three-hour interviews. Partners were not interviewed together
since this might have resulted in the couples jointly presenting to the
interviewer a united front, a public version of their marriage. They also
decided against interviewing each marriage partner on separate occasions since it was possible that the first subject might give the other
partner some forewarning as to the questions that were being asked.
Further, interviewing the partners separately, but simultaneously,

meant that the interviewers were able to explore possible differences in understandings of marriage between men and women.

The interviews were taped and transcribed and then began the long and difficult process of analysis. The interviewers were not simply recording opinions or describing marriages; they were seeking to provide an analysis which, while being true to the participants own understandings of how they saw and experienced marriage, linked with wider discussions about the nature of marriage in modern Britain. This move beyond description, in their words, involved '. . . a leap of the sociological imagination' (ibid., p.48).

Principal Findings

Small-scale qualitative studies of this kind do not produce 'findings' in the conventional sense. Certainly, some descriptive generalisations do emerge from this study. Thus we find that over half of the sample began their married life in their own accommodation (ibid., p.114) and that only three brides said that they were virgins on their wedding night (ibid., p.77). But these are not the most important themes to emerge from this study.

More important is the meaning that might be given to these facts and how they might be linked to other generalisations that run through the study. Thus the finding about accommodation is significant when it is linked to the importance that couples give to the idea of developing a life on their own. The finding about previous sexual experience can be linked to more general points about how sexual intimacy is valued as part of the marriage relationship.

What are important, therefore, are the themes that run through the work as a whole and three of the most important are as follows:

(i) *Planners, Venturers and Roamers*

Small-scale studies of this kind help us to understand social institutions as dynamic processes. Marriage in particular has a sense of change and development built into it. However, this idea of process should not be seen as the following of well-established and laid down patterns, as we might find in an occupational career. The authors describe modern courtship as a 'trail' rather than as a 'career', often a haphazard trail, and this sense of movement runs through all aspects of the study (ibid., p.73). Processes through courtship and marriage are not all identical and the authors attempted to elaborate distinctive, although overlapping, types of movements through early marriage. Further, images of the future shape present plans, understandings and expectations. A sense of the future, in fact, provided the authors with the title of their book:

> Getting married is where it all starts. You're not a kid any more, you're branching out on your own – it's the beginning of the rest of your life. (A husband quoted, ibid., p.199)

This sense of the future was not uniform across all the couples. Some individuals seemed to have a sense of planning for the future that went well beyond the necessary planning for the wedding. They had clear ideas of what would be the most suitable form of accommodation, of when to start having children and perhaps even extended their vision on to retirement. These people were described by the authors as *planners*. The remaining people, *the non-planners* could be divided into two further categories. Firstly, there were those individuals described as *venturers*. They seemed to recognise that it was not possible to plan every detail for the future and accepted that there were many uncertainties ahead. They accepted that marriage, like life itself, was something of a gamble, and were prepared to accept this. The second set of non-planners were described as *roamers*. These appeared to be characterised by a relative lack of a sense of purpose or direction, reacting to outside pressures or circumstances rather than seeking to take some kind of initiative. The *venturers* were prepared to accept uncertainty and perhaps even to welcome the challenge that this provided; the *roamers* seemed to be more fatalistic or resigned in the face of uncertainty.

Individuals are not necessarily fixed into these orientations. They may shift from one pattern to another over time, perhaps as perceived circumstances change. Couples may be made up of individuals with different orientations to the future. Thus, for example, a planning husband may be married to a roaming wife. (See p.13, for some further examples.)

(ii) *The Importance of Gender*

In one famous discussion, the American sociologist, Jessie Bernard, argued that we should not talk of a single marriage but of 'his' and 'her' marriages (Bernard, 1972). Like Bernard, the present authors felt that husbands and wives would tend to have different perspectives on marriage and sought to explore the importance of gender differences at all stages of their research. They found that it was often an important source of difference, probably more important than social class in most cases. This was most obvious in the division of labour within the home. At this early stage of marriage, much time is spent in establishing domestic routines, the organization of time and the distribution of tasks that need to be done in and around the home. At this stage in their lives, most wives were also in full-time employment. The most common pattern of division of labour in the home identified by the authors was what they called the 'neo-traditional' pattern. This differed from the 'traditional' distinction between the 'breadwinning' husband and the home-based 'housewife' in that both partners were in paid employment and that, while the wife did most of the domestic labour in the home, she expected, and usually got, some 'help' from her husband. Half the men and women held the view that this neo-traditional division was the most appropriate. More men than women held the traditional view. Very few held an egalitarian view of complete sharing as an ideal, while roughly a third of the husbands and wives held an 'equitable' view, one that accepted that husbands and wives might do different things in the home but that the overall *burden* should be shared equitably.

Thus there was an expectation that housework was more a matter for wives, even if they might reasonably expect some help from their husbands. However, the fact that most of the wives were in full-time employment meant that their total work burden was often very heavy:

> These newly-wed women were constantly in a state of tension: between wanting to run their homes to high standards and having to fulfil outside employment commitments: between wanting husbands who would help and thereby relieve the pressure, and wanting to prove that they were good housewives and keep their own territory. (ibid., 1988, p.136)

Despite the fact that both partners usually worked outside the home, they tended to assume that the employment of the husband had priority. Future parenthood was expected to sharpen the difference between partners and, presumably, to strengthen the belief in, and the practice of, the neo-traditional division of labour in the home.

This focus on gender differences runs throughout the study and provides one of the main themes. It enters into the heart of the understanding of the marital relationship itself. Thus, while both partners believed in the importance of confiding and sharing problems, the emphasis tended to be different for women and men. Women saw these confidings as important for airing *feelings*, while men saw these sessions as an occasion for working out *solutions* as part of a process of joint problem-solving. At the most general level, the very basis of 'togetherness' was seen in different ways:

> Most (though not all) men seek a *life in common* with their wives, a home life, a physical and psychological base; somewhere and someone to set out from and return to.
>
> But, for nearly all the wives, their desired marriage was a *common life* with an empathetic partner, who was to provide both material and emotional security. (ibid., p.179, their emphasis)

(iii) *Identity and Stability in Marriage*

Another study of marriage distinguished between the themes of 'identity' and 'stability' (Askham, 1984). Identity stressed the idea of individuality and developing one's personality in and through marriage. Stability stressed the marital relationship itself, as a basis of equilibrium both for individuals and for society as a whole. This kind of tension between thinking of 'me' and thinking of 'we' seemed to be present even in these earliest months of marriage. It was not so much a question of submerging oneself in a couple relationship, but rather one of seeing a new 'me' develop as a consequence of becoming married. One respondent, a young bride, expressed it in these terms:

I want to be *me* first, as well as being married. (ibid., p. 163)

Many of the quarrels, arguments and tiffs that took place in these early months could be seen as attempts to work out this tension between a desire to be a separate individual and a desire to accept the constraints, as well as to enjoy the benefits, that being in a couple relationship provided. The authors note that there is a widespread belief, echoed in public statements by clergy or in media treatments of marriages in the public gaze, that marriage ought to be a relationship in the deepest sense of taking over individual differences. Yet the day to day reality of marriage, the tension between home and work and between men and women seems to say something different:

Modern marriage is a paradox. The language of marital relationships denies differences, the reality of married life defies sameness. (ibid., p.194)

Discussion

While this study received some attention in the weightier newspapers, discussion in academic journals has, so far at least, been surprisingly sparse. Whatever the reason for this relative lack of scholarly review, this should not detract from the real merits of this work.

There are some points that deserve further attention. It contains a good discussion of the use of joint, but separate, interviews as a key element in this mode of qualitative methodology. However, what is perhaps lacking is a sense of the interview itself as a social process. Most of the quotations used are brief and, if the interviews were indeed conversations, the reader gets very little sense of the exchanges that constitute such conversations and which produce the quoted passages. The interviewers themselves remain very much in the background and we have little sense of how their age, gender, class or marital status entered into, and influenced, the interviewing process.

It can be argued that there is relatively little systematic exploration of differences within the sample, other than gender. It is claimed that this is a more important source of difference in response than class, but this may to some extent reflect that measures of class based upon the husband's occupation (which the authors themselves have reservations about) may be too crude to explore differences within marriage. Joint measures, taking the occupations of both the husband and the wife, although more complex, could have been used, as could others, such as housing or education. In fact there are very few references to class in the main body of the text, although they do note that semi-skilled and unskilled husbands were more likely to refuse to take part in the interviews (ibid., p.42). Hence, those working-class couples that were selected might have been closer in values and attitudes to the middle-class respondents than to those of the population as a whole. Further, there is no exploration of the possible impact of 'cross-class marriages', where the social status of one partner is higher than that of the other (see Macrae, 1986).

Class is not the only social difference that could have been explored. One factor, for a long time considered to be important in understanding marital behaviour, is to do with social network (Bott, 1957). This recognises that married couples rarely, if ever, exist on their own but can be placed in wider networks of kin, neighbours and friends. These networks, which vary considerably in terms of extent, density and importance may influence a person's understanding of, or response to, marriage. Thus it is possible that the *planners* lived their lives in networks which gave considerable support to the idea and the practice of planning in marriage as in other areas of life. The authors describe some important differences in attitudes to, and expectations surrounding, marriage, but do not take us very far in understanding the sources of such differences.

There are, finally, the ever-present problems of the representativeness of the sample. How far is it possible to generalise about 'marriage in Britain today' from a relatively small sample of London-based couples who were married in church? However, since the authors are less concerned with presenting the reader with firm 'facts' about marriage and more concerned with exploring a range of themes and meanings that might be given to modern marriage, this sampling problem is perhaps less troublesome than it might have been.

Conclusion

This study is an important exploration of the everyday world of marriage in modern Britain. Much of the material is undramatic and unsensational but the study is far from dull and it is likely that through it most readers will recognise something of their own marriages, or the marriages of others they know. It demonstrates how close, largely qualitative, research illuminates everyday domestic life. As a study which is clearly influenced by both interactionism and recent feminist scholarship, it throws light on issues beyond the immediate experiences of the couples under examination.

One such issue is to do with the character of marriage in a modern society. Marriage may now be seen less frequently as a major legal and social institution, a fact underlined by the increased possibility and greater incidence of divorce. But couples still have high expectations of it as a major adult relationship. With all its uncertainties and insecurities, especially around issues of gender, it remains a central concern in the lives of many individuals.

Bibliography

Askham, J. (1984), *Identity and Stability in Marriage*, Cambridge
    University Press.
Bernard, J. (1972), *The Future of Marriage*, New York, Wales
    Publishing.
Bott, E. (1957), *Family and Social Network*, London, Tavistock.
Macrae, S. (1986), *Cross-Class Families: A Study of Wives' Occupa-
    tional Superiority*, Oxford, Clarendon Press.
Mansfield, P. and Collard, J. (1988), *The Beginning of the Rest of Your
    Life?*, Basingstoke, Macmillan.

Appendices

Table 1.1 Marriages: by type

United Kingdom   Thousands and percentages

	1961	1971	1976	1981	1986	1989	1990
Marriages (thousands)							
First marriage for both partners	340	369	282	263	254	252	241
First marriage for one partner only							
Bachelor/divorced woman	11	21	30	32	34	35	34
Bachelor/widow	5	4	4	3	2	2	2
Spinster/divorced man	12	24	32	36	38	38	37
Spinster/widower	8	5	4	3	2	2	2
Second (or subsequent) marriage for both partners							
Both divorced	5	17	34	44	48	50	47
Both widowed	10	10	10	7	6	5	5
Divorced man/widow	3	4	5	5	4	4	4
Divorced woman/widower	3	5	5	5	5	5	4
Total marriages	397	459	406	398	394	392	375
Remarriages[1] as a percentage of all marriages	14	20	31	34	35	36	36
Remarriages[1] of the divorced as a percentage of all marriages	9	15	26	31	33	34	34

[1] Remarriage for one or both partners.
Source: Central Statistical Office (1993), *Social Trends*, London, HMSO (Table 2.12,
p.29)

Table 1.2 Divorce[1]

	1961	1971	1976	1981	1986	1987	1988	1989	1990
Petitions filed[2] (thousands)									
England & Wales	32	111	145	170	180	183	183	185	192
Decrees nisi granted (thousands)									
England & Wales	27	89	132	148	153	150	155	152	158
Decrees absolute granted (thousands)									
England & Wales	25	74	127	146	154	151	153	151	153
Scotland	2	5	9	10	13	12	11	12	12
Northern Ireland	–	–	1	1	2	2	2	2	2
United Kingdom	27	80	136	157	168	165	166	164	168
Persons divorcing per thousand married people									
England & Wales	2.1	6.0	10.1	11.9	12.9	12.7	12.8	12.7	12.9
Percentage of divorces where one or both partners had been divorced in an immediately previous marriage									
England & Wales	9.3	8.8	11.6	17.1	23.2	23.5	24.0	24.7	24.9

[1] This table includes annulment throughout. See Appendix, Part 2: Divorce.
[2] Estimates based on 100 per cent of petitions at the Principle Registry together with a 2 month sample of county court petitions (March and September).
Source: Central Statistical Office (1993), *Social Trends*, London, HMSO (Table 2.14, p.30)

Examples of planners, venturers and roamers

A planning husband, married to a roaming wife:

'I thought a lot about married life before we got married and really it's how I thought about it - how I planned it, really . . .'

'We've got a plan kind of thing - wait a few years to start a family - we've thought about our plans for the future.' (Mr Browning)

'It's Nigel that wants to wait longer. *I* would have a baby next year because I love children, and that was my first feeling, but as Nigel says, when you get your own home you realise the bills and the money you have to pay out . . . so we will wait and get the house the way we want it and do the things we want to do, get some money behind us, like Nigel says. And that's what *I'd* like to do now.' (Mrs Browning)

A venturing husband, married to a roaming wife:

'We realised that we loved each other and we got on very well and really enjoyed each other's company and marriage seemed to be the logical conclusion – so we got married.'

'Not that we are particularly worried about her getting pregnant, but we weren't aiming for her to get pregnant now.' (Mr Roberts)

'. . . I knew I wanted to marry him but I didn't know if I wanted to so quickly. He got very impatient – if he wants to do something he can't wait. He's such a sure and confident person. I wish *I* was like that.' (Mrs Roberts)

A roamer wife, married to a venturing husband:

'We didn't really plan – no definite date set for the wedding . . . just see how it goes . . . drifted along I suppose. Andy got fed up on his own . . . so we decided to marry.'

'If I started a family tomorrow it wouldn't worry me – I'm not fussy either way.' (Mrs Slater)

'He's easy going, if he comes home and there's no tea he'll go out and get something – or wash a shirt for himself. He's generous, would give you anything, always in the same mood, never miserable. I don't think he ever worries.' (Mrs Slater)

Quotations from Mansfield and Collard (1988), pp.213–221. All emphases in original.

2

Financial Arrangements within Marriage

Jan Pahl (1989), *Money and Marriage*, Basingstoke, Macmillan.

Celia Lury

Introduction

In contemporary society money is a medium of exchange, not only in the conventional economic, but also in a social and ideological, sense. The sharing of resources within households occupies a crucial intersection between the economic and the social, and between the economy outside the household and that within it. Yet very little is known about it. Jan Pahl's study provides much-needed information about the processes which take place within households between the earning and the spending of income. Its central thesis is that money is a tracer of power relations within marriage and it explores the extent to which the different economic situations of husbands and wives are reflected in differences between 'his' marriage and 'her' marriage. It also considers the implications of different forms of intervention by the state in the lives of married couples.

Marriage, the Household and Money

In many forms of economic and social analysis, including not only academic and market research but also government studies, households are commonly considered basic economic units. Households are assumed to behave as if they were 'the unit' of consumption, rather than as one distribution point among others for individual consumption. By treating it as though it were a single unit, without conflicts of interest between its constituent members, the household has become a sort of black box, within which the transfer of resources between earners and spenders has been rendered invisible:

> By a heroic simplification the separate identities of men and women are merged into the concept of the household. The inner conflicts and compromises of the household are not explored. (Galbraith, quoted by Pahl, p.4)

15

However, for some time now, the assumption that there are no internal divisions has been challenged by feminists who have pointed to the tensions between the couple and the individual, and between the two individuals who make up the couple.

Pahl's study seeks to explore how the *economic* aspects of married life contribute to the very different ways in which men and women experience marriage.

These differences are sustained by a complex of inter-related factors. Until the late nineteenth century the position had been that, under common law, marriage meant that husband and wife became one person: the legal existence of the woman was incorporated into that of her husband. This implied that any property which a woman possessed or was entitled to at the time of the marriage, and any property which she became entitled to after it, became her husband's to control. In 1882, the Married Women's Property Act gave married women the same rights over property as men and unmarried women. It can be seen as the greatest transfer of resources from married men to married women which has ever taken place; it is thus as important a date in the history of the reallocation of property as the dissolution of the monasteries. However, though it can be seen as a great victory for feminists, and for women, it did not achieve anything like equality because it did little to alter the ongoing financial dependence of wives on their husbands.

In contemporary British society, this dependence continues as a result of differential rates of pay and state allowances, the barring of women, formally or informally, from the better paid jobs, a lack of public child care and an ideology of dependent femininity. As Pahl's study shows it is also a consequence of the internal dynamics in households.

Research Design

The main aim of the study was to gain a better understanding of financial management within households and to investigate the significance of different allocative systems for individual members of households. The study was concerned not only with documenting existing patterns of allocation of money but also with analysing the social and economic processes which shaped those patterns and which might lead to changes over time. It was also intended to reveal relationships between patterns of allocation of money and other dimensions in the lives of husbands and wives, such as deference and authority, dependence and independence, and the relative power of husband and wife.

The completed study eventually involved interviews with 102 married couples, each with at least one child under 16. Health centre records were used to get access to a near complete population of couples with children in Pahl's locality; from these, a random sample was selected and approached with a request for an interview. Despite a relatively low response rate (52%), the couples who took part in the study were reasonably similar to the larger population of married couples with dependent children in Britain. Each couple was interviewed first together and then separately. This strategy was a response to problems thrown up by previous research. Many studies of marriage and family life are based on interviews with one spouse or one family member, usually the wife since she is more likely to be at home and more amenable to being interviewed; they are thus likely to be one-sided accounts. The technique of employing both joint and separate interviews was designed to ensure that the differences between 'his' and 'her' marriage would be properly expressed in the data.

A structured questionnaire was used in the interviews, with verbatim comments noted down at the time and only a small number of tape-recorded interviews. The joint interviews collected information about the household as a whole and the couple as a unit. Questions were asked about all members of the household and their employment, if any. Using a check list of items on which the family might have to spend money, the couple were asked who actually paid for each item. A series of open-ended questions was concerned with how money was organized within the household, and more general questions explored subjective evaluation of standards of living and attitudes to money. The separate interviews investigated these and other issues, but from the points of view of the individual spouses.

The questions were designed to collect information about individual and collective expenditure in order to investigate the extent of shared standards of living within the household. They were also concerned with the question of who exercised control and management. *Control* is concerned with decisions such as what type of allocative system should be adopted within the household, which spouse should have the final say on major financial decisions, and with the extent to which spouses have control over personal spending money of their own and joint money. *Management* is concerned with putting into operation the particular allocative system which the couple have adopted.

Principal Findings

(i) *Systems of allocation*

Of the 102 couples, half the women and most of the men were in paid employment at the time of the interview. All the women were in receipt of child benefit and all the men who were not in employment received either unemployment benefit, invalidity benefit or supplementary benefit (now income support). Thus every individual who took part in the study had some form of income, whether as wages, salary or social security payment. About half the sample also had some savings, held either jointly or individually. However, as *Table 2.1*, p.23 shows, the conditions of employment were rather different for men and women.

In general, men worked longer hours, with 70% doing paid work for 40 or more hours each week, compared with 16% of the women. Compared with the men, the women were likely to be paid weekly rather than monthly, and they were much more likely to be paid in cash; half of the women, but three-quarters of the men, received their earnings as a cheque or direct debit to a bank account. Not surprisingly, there were substantial differences between husbands and wives in the amounts they earned. The take-home pay of the wives varied from £21 to £81 per week, while that of the men varied from £29 to £300 per week (see *Table 2.2*, p.23). Income here includes: take-home pay, child benefits, earnings from second jobs, interest on savings, gifts from relatives, loans and gambling wins.

These tables show very clearly the inequality between men and women in the labour market. (At the time of the interviews the mean wages of full-time women workers were 66% of those of male workers (Central Statistical Office, 1986).) Women's enforced responsibility for housework and the care of children exacerbates this inequality. The resulting disparity in income between men and women means that in the great majority of marriages there has to be some sharing of economic resources if the women and children are not to have a lower standard of living than the men. Every couple has to devise some arrangement by which this transfer of resources can take place. Though many may never consciously decide to organize their finances in one way or another, there was found to be a describable system of money management in every case.

On the basis of her analysis of the questionnaire, Pahl distinguished four different ways of organizing money, although she is careful to note that, in reality, the four different allocative systems shade into each other. She used two main criteria for identifying systems of allocation of money. These were, first, the extent to which each partner had *access* to the main source of money coming into the household, usually the husband's wage or social security payment, and second, the extent to which he or she had *responsibility* for managing household expenditure.

The first of the four systems is *wife management* or the *whole wage system*. Here one partner, in Britain almost always the wife, is responsible for managing all the finances of the household and is also responsible for all the expenditure, except for the personal spending money of the other partner, as part of her household chores. There are several different versions of wife management; probably the most common form is that in which husband hands his pay packet to his wife (to which she will add her earnings if she is in paid employment), either taking out his personal spending money before he does so, or receiving it back from her. In a variation of this, the husband, although he expects the wife to be responsible for making ends meet, sees himself as having the right to take money back from her. This variation makes visible the power relations underpinning this system: although the wife is responsible for expenditure, this responsibility is one of her household chores and is carried out under conditions of dependence.

The second of the four systems is the *allowance system*. Married couples who adopt this system typically see themselves as having separate spheres of responsibility in financial matters. In the most common form of this system the husband gives his wife a set amount every week or month, to which she usually adds her own earnings if she has any. She is then responsible for paying for specific items of household expenditure, while the rest of the money remains in the control of the husband and he pays for other items. Thus he has access to the main source of income, while she only has access to that part of it which he chooses to give her for housekeeping.

The third of the four systems is the *pooling system* or *shared management*. Pooling couples have a joint account or common kitty into which both incomes are paid and from which they both draw. Thus both have access to the income entering the household and expenditure responsibilities are more or less shared. Shared management is often represented as expressing a commitment to a partnership model of marriage, though there are instances where there is very clearly a senior and junior partner. Asked 'do you feel you ever have to justify spending money?', one husband said 'no', while the wife replied:

> Sometimes. He'll moan when £40 has gone and I have to explain it to him. But I get what I want. If I want a dress I'll get it – I'll get round him slowly afterwards – I'll hide it at the back of the wardrobe till I've won him round! (Pahl, 1989, p.74)

It appears, then, that shared management is associated with increased accountability for wives but not for husbands. Pahl comments that 'sharing rarely compensates for the lower earning capacity and the financial dependence of married women' (ibid., p. 74).

The last of the four systems is the *independent management system*. The essential characteristic of this system is that both partners have an income and that neither has access to all the household funds. Each partner is responsible for specific items of expenditure, and though these responsibilities may change over time, the principle of separate control over income and separate responsibility for expenditure is maintained. In general terms, Pahl concludes that more couples now share the management of household income compared with 30 years ago; however, there are still many marriages where husbands control and manage finances and wives' access to money is severely limited.

(ii) *Finance and power in marriage*

Pahl then goes on to develop explanations for these patterns by analysing correlations between financial arrangements and other aspects of the lives of married couples. A correlation is not, of course, the same as a cause. Yet the existence of overlapping correlations is used by Pahl to suggest patterns of causality. She found that while explanations couched in terms of practicalities or psychological explanations were more commonly presented in interviews than other explanations, the socio-economic circumstances of peoples' lives and the ideologies which shaped their views of the world often had greater explanatory power.

Different variables become significant in different circumstances. Household income is an important variable when income is low: when money is short, and therefore managing it is a demanding chore rather than a source of power or pleasure, then typically women manage and control finances. At higher income levels, the source of that income becomes important. If only the husband is in employment he tends to control the money, and to delegate management of a part of it to his wife. The higher the proportion of household income contributed by the wife the more likely it is that she will control finances, although overall control may still reflect the relative earning power and the economic contribution of each of the two individuals involved.

Pahl also found that adherence to the ideology of 'the family', in which an ideal of a male breadwinner and dependent wife and children is upheld, is a crucial factor, but one whose effect is variable. For example, it is often used as a justification: wives are seen as better at management when money is short, while husbands are defined as financially knowledgeable when there is more money and when the wife's work is unpaid. Pahl thus concludes that, as *Figure 2.3*, p. 24 illustrates, it is not always clear what is cause and what is effect.

Data from the interviews supports the thesis that there are clear differences between 'his' and 'her' marriages. It suggests, for example, that there is a discrepancy between theory and practice in the attitudes of husband and wife to earned income. Both partners were likely to define the husband's income as earmarked for collective expenditure; yet in practice many husbands did not make all their income available to their family, especially in households where wives were given an allowance for housekeeping. By comparison, wives' incomes tended to be defined, especially by husbands, as earmarked for individual expenditure; yet in practice most wives used their income to buy things for their family, or added their earnings to the housekeeping money.

The amount spent on housekeeping was related both to the level of household income and to the amount contributed by each partner. However, while the husband contributed most *absolutely* to house-keeping, since on average his income was four times as great as that of his wife, the wife contributed most *relatively*. More concretely, if the incomes of wife and husband rose by the same amount, 28% of her increase would go to housekeeping compared with 16% of his. Put starkly, wives do not have the same rights as husbands to control the money they earn. These findings have important implications for social policy, and especially for income maintenance schemes aimed at providing financial support to families. They suggest that channelling payments via women is likely to be a more effective way of maintaining children at a given standard of living than channelling the same sum via men.

Husbands and wives also had different expectations regarding leisure. Husbands were more likely actually to have money for personal spending and for leisure than were wives. Yet, typically, husbands over-estimated the amounts wives spent on leisure, while wives under-estimated how much their husbands spent. In general, wives' rights to leisure seemed less secure and 'leisure' sometimes involved domestic work; thus when one husband was asked what leisure activities his wife had, he replied: 'Ironing, sewing, reading'.

Evaluation

This section of Pahl's analysis thus shows that though financial arrangements within marriage may take an economic form, their significance cannot be understood without taking account of social structures, processes and meanings. Pahl herself locates her own work within a broadly quantitative (and, by implication, in opposition to a qualitative) approach, setting considerable store by the size and representativeness of her sample. Yet, as she herself notes, typologies of allocative systems group together widely varying arrangements and in reality different allocative systems shade into each other. These ambiguities call in question the validity of the extensive comparisons Pahl makes between different allocative systems as to patterns of personal spending, the ratio of housekeeping money to overall income, perceptions of control of finance and so on. In addition, Pahl sometimes correlates categories that are not analytically distinct, complicating her use of correlations to imply causality. In any case, the dichotomy between quantitative and qualitative paradigms is rather starkly drawn; a fuller analysis of the responses to her structured questionnaire would have allowed her to throw yet more light on the tensions surrounding money management in marriage than the predominantly statistical analysis reveals.

It is the analysis of these ambiguities that would allow an understanding of the full complexity of the underlying power relations to emerge. These are often left unexplicated; for example, there is little discussion of how the couples came to agree (or, and this might itself be worth studying, if not agree at least accept) the allocative systems they adopted. Furthermore, as Pahl herself notes, money is not the only resource which is exchanged within households. Other resources include time and space, as well as skill, knowledge and emotional labour. Marriage is not only a site for the distribution of resources; it is also a primary site of heterosexual relations, mothering and sexual violence. Pahl's analysis abstracts allocative systems from the complex and sometimes conflictual relationship which is described as marriage. It does not, for example, consider how declarations of love may influence or shape the distribution of economic resources, or how the experience of full-time housework can undermine women's self-confidence and estimation of their own value.

Conclusion

Marriage is sometimes described as a 'conjugal contract', a description which implies an equal and agreed bargain between husband and wife, in which financial support is exchanged for domestic work and child care. Yet, the contract is not between equals, since few women earn enough to support a husband and children and few men would agree to accept the loss of life time earnings experienced by most wives and mothers. Furthermore, the widespread incidence of domestic violence suggests that the contract is often enforced rather than freely chosen. This is the point that Carole Pateman makes when she talks of marriage as a key element in *The Sexual Contract* by which she means the general power that men exercise over women. She suggests that the marriage contract is claimed to be the product of free social choices, but like other contracts about property in the person, it in fact 'generates a political right in the form of relations of domination and subordination' (Pateman, 1988, p.8).

Pahl's study clearly shows that the rights which husbands acquire through the marriage contract, though no longer as extensive as in the mid-nineteenth century when wives could not legally own property, still include those to economic control of household resources. While a women is likely to contribute a higher proportion of her earnings to housekeeping than her husband, her income is still likely to be regarded as marginal; a man is likely to contribute a lower proportion of his earnings but he still feels justified in spending more than his wife on leisure. In short, the study shows that the links between money, gender and power hold inside the household as well as outside it. It raises fundamental questions as to who decides how household income is to be divided, who spends it and who benefits from expenditure. And it reveals gender inequalities in the control, management and distribution of household resources. It thus shows that gender inequality in the wider society reinforces, and is in turn reinforced by, gender inequality within the household.

Bibliography and Further Reading

Delphy, C. and Leonard, D. (1992), *Familiar Exploitation: A New Analysis of Marriage in Contemporary Western Societies*, Cambridge, Polity.

Finch, J. (1989), *Family Obligations and Social Change*, Cambridge, Polity.

Kerr, M. and Charles, N. 'Servers and providers: the distribution of food within the family' in *Sociological Review*, Vol.34, No.1, pp.115–157.

Leonard, D. 'Women in the family: companions or caretakers?' in Beechey, V. and Whitelegg, E. (eds.) (1986), *Women in Britain Today*, Milton Keynes, Open University Press.

Morris, L. and Ruane, S. (1989), *Household Finance Management and the Labour Market*, Aldershot, Gower.

Pateman, C. (1988), *The Sexual Contract*, Cambridge, Polity.

Appendices

Table 2.1 Conditions of employment of study couples

		Women (N=51) %	Men (N=90) %
Hours worked weekly:	Less than 29	69	—
	30–39	14	30
	40–49	12	37
	50+	4	33
Wages/salary paid:	weekly	68	53
	monthly	23	42
	other	9	4
Paid in the form of:	cash	48	25
	cheque/direct debit	52	75
Deductions from pay for:	private pension	8	59
	health insurance	4	19
	union dues	13	39
Fringe benefits as:	help with travel	15	52
	goods	33	42
	tools supplied	8	33
	sporting facilities	6	34
	Christmas bonus	27	47

(Pahl, 1989, Table 5.1, p.64)

Table 2.2 Total net income of study couples

		Women %	Men %
Income per week:	up to £19	34	—
	£19–£57	49	6
	£58–£95	15	23
	£96–£134	2	32
	£135–£172	—	23
	£173+	—	17
	Total per cent	100	100
	Total number	102	102

(ibid., Table 5.2, p.65)

Figure 2.3 Money and marriage: a model

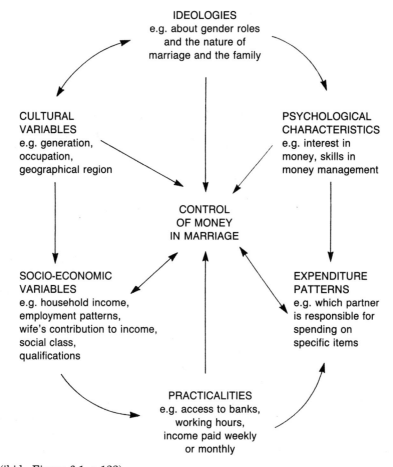

(ibid., Figure 6.1, p.122)

3

Households and Resources

Sandra Wallman (1984), *Eight London Households*, London, Tavistock.

Janet Finch

Sociological Perspectives

The basic unit of daily living in most societies is the household – people who live under the same roof and who share a common life. In Britain today most people do live as part of such a 'group' household. Except in old age very few people live alone, as single-person households, though the number of people who make a positive choice to do so is probably growing.

So the group household is the common way of organizing daily life for the majority of people in Britain. Usually this group consists of people who are related to each other as parents and children, as sexual partners, as brothers and sisters, though of course households sometimes also include people who are not related. Whatever their relationship, official definitions tend to count people as part of the same household if they live under the same roof and share some common expenses. In this sense the household can be seen as an economic unit, not just a collection of individuals. Resources come in to the unit through different routes (wages earned by various household members, benefits received from the state, gifts in money or in goods, for example), and can be used in different ways to benefit one or all of the members of the household (to buy food, to pay for heating, to improve the standard of comfort in the home, and so on).

So how do households work as economic units? How are resources used within these units? How does this affect the standard of living and the quality of life of different household members? *Eight London Households* sets out to answer these questions by examining in detail how households operate as 'resource systems', that is, as economic units which deploy various resources to the benefit of their members. Its main link to sociological debates therefore is in relation to *households and families*, and to understanding how they work in practice.

In addition to this, the study has a focus on *locality*. Sandra Wallman, the author, thought that it was important to see households in their local context, if we wish to understand what resources are available to them and how those resources are used. She and her team chose to investigate households living in a particular locality in an inner city setting. This meant that the households they studied were living in circumstances where managing resources, and creating a good standard of living for household members, were likely to be quite difficult. So the book also contributes to sociological debates about *problems of inner city living*.

In order to develop a detailed study of households, Wallman found it necessary to specify the range of 'resources' which households can use. She decided to include the following in her analysis:

(1) housing
(2) services
(3) goods and money
(4) time
(5) information
(6) identity

The importance of the first three is obvious: all households need adequate shelter, money to buy food and other necessities, and access to basic services (such as electricity or rubbish collection) if their members are to thrive.

The other three 'resources' which Sandra Wallman discusses are less obvious, but also important. The way in which family members use *time* (especially time which is not spent doing paid work) can affect the way in which other resources are used. An illustration here can help us to understand the importance of time, and also shows what Sandra Wallman means by 'managing' resources. Baking your own bread and cakes can save money on the shopping bill. Your own time (a resource) is used to make the most of your money (another resource). But using time in this way may mean that you can give less attention to your children. Which of these is preferable in creating a good standard of living for the household? There is, of course, no correct answer to that question. It is likely that different choices will be made in different households, depending partly on what other options each household has. We need information about the total picture before we can understand fully why members of one household decide that baking their own bread is the best use of the available resources, and another household decides that it is not.

Similar arguments can be made about the other types of resource which Wallman mentions. By referring to *information* as a resource, she reminds us that people often need certain knowledge to obtain extra resources, or to make the most of what they already have – for example, knowing where good food can be bought cheaply, knowing how to apply for housing benefit to help pay your rent, or knowing where are the local employers who might be interested in employing someone with your particular skills. If you do not know these things yourself, it helps to know someone else who will tell you.

Wallman's idea that *identity* is a resource is perhaps the most difficult to grasp. She suggests that, for example, being seen as a 'local' Battersea person, someone who belongs there, is an identity which can be useful in certain circumstances, perhaps making it more likely that a local employer will give you a job. Another important identity for some LARA residents is an ethnic identity, as Caribbean or west African, for example. Again, this may give access to other resources – information, time, even money – which would not be available to a white person.

Wallman's model of the household is therefore complex, focussing on how resources of all six types are managed. The task required data, in depth, on household processes and experiences.

The Study

Eight London Households reports the findings of the final stage of a larger study, all of which was about daily life in south London. The research was conducted in one small area of Battersea, eight streets in total, which constituted the Louvaine Area Residents' Association (LARA). At the time of the study, LARA had many of the classic features of inner city areas: a good deal of movement both in and out of the district in the recent past, housing in need of renovation and some recently renovated, a higher than average proportion of the population who were – or whose parents had been – migrants from New Commonwealth countries.

The earlier part of this research (reported in another book: see Wallman et al., 1982) was based on questionnaire surveys, initially of all the houses in LARA, and then a further and detailed questionnaire study of a sub-sample. However the findings discussed in *Eight London Households* are based on more intensive study of a further sub-sample of eight households. This approach was necessary because the researchers wanted to build up a detailed picture of what resources are available to households in this type of area, and of different ways in which those resources are managed. Members of these eight households were interviewed about their daily lives, about their past and present experiences of household organization, about how they coped with various crises which they had experienced. They were asked to give detailed job histories. They filled in time charts which showed exactly how they spent their time over a given 24 hour period. They were also asked to fill in 'network maps'.

The idea of the network map is a particular innovation in this study and yields some interesting information about *resources potentially available* to the households. The idea here is that having lots of contacts with people outside the household should improve access to information, practical assistance and help in finding work, thus making best use of resources. This should be especially true if the contacts are 'close' in two senses – geographically close, and close in terms of affection or liking. By plotting the network maps of the households she studied, Sandra Wallman was able to test these ideas. The form in which the network maps were plotted is given in *Figure 3.1, p.33.* The first chart shows the map for plotting geographical closeness, whilst the second shows the network map for 'affective' closeness. Wallman's interviewees were asked to fill in the names of all their contacts in the appropriate space on each chart. Note that each chart has a section for including people who, although in some ways may be 'close', nonetheless are also sometimes experienced as 'difficult'. Such people, though well known to the household, may be less useful than others in resource terms.

By these various methods, the research team built up a large amount of detail on each household. But how were the eight households chosen for this part of the study? Mainly they were chosen because they were all rather similar – people with similar jobs, similar incomes, all with young children, with other relatives living nearby, and all having been resident in the area for at least five years. So they were very similar in terms of the resources likely to be available to the household. In addition, all of them had experienced some kind of 'normal' family crisis in the last twelve months (for example, a birth, a death, redundancy). This enabled the researchers to investigate how the household had used its available resources to see it through this crisis.

A study based on as few as eight cases is rare. But by selecting them carefully, and by studying them intensively in this way, Sandra Wallman and her team were able to produce a piece of research which shows that there can be wide variation in the management of daily life, even in eight households whose circumstances are superficially very similar.

Principal Findings

This is a rich and detailed study, with many interesting findings. It would be impossible to report all of them here. However, there are three main themes which are important for understanding how household resources are managed:

> (i) *Households do manage their affairs effectively for much of the time, even those who live in inner cities, and in difficult circumstances*

This study was set deliberately in the inner city, where normally it is assumed that people live difficult, unsettled and impoverished lives. None of the eight households was well off, and all of them had been through some very difficult times. Yet all were managing to bring up their children, and to create a lifestyle for themselves, which they regarded as satisfactory. Sandra Wallman argues therefore that it is wrong to see inner city living as necessarily problematic. An inner city environment can offer practical possibilities for a decent life for those who are able to, and who want to, manage it.

This point is made in a particularly interesting way in relation to two of the households in the study – the Abrahams' and the Charles'. Both of these consisted of single black women, bringing up young children alone. The image of the black single mother, living in the inner city, normally invites the label 'problem family', says Wallman. But her study shows that each of them, in very different ways, was succeeding in keeping a home together and in fulfilling her own central aim of being a good mother. Cynthia Abrahams was particularly good at building up and using her networks, of which she had three – one based on her job, one based on neighbourhood ties, and one based on links with other people from the African country where she was born. She put a lot into these contacts, often spending much of her weekends entertaining friends and relatives. But she also felt well supported, both practically and emotionally, by her wide range of contacts.

(ii) *Households can and do use a wide range of resources to the benefit of their members*

The design of this study makes visible the complex ways in which households work, and the range of resources which people do use. Making something of a play on words, Sandra Wallman says that households are indeed 'resourceful'. This is seen in particular when faced with a crisis, where people will try to use a wide range of resources available to them through their access to time, information, identity, money and services. This does not mean that every problem can be easily solved. But it does mean that people have a number of avenues which they try to explore, often piecing together a solution from different resources. Partly this involves working through the various possibilities represented by each person's network map, and thus making the most of the available resources to the benefit of household members.

A good example of this is the description of how Olive Charles – one of the black single mothers – handled a crisis in which she had to make arrangements to have her children cared for whilst she went into hospital for a serious operation. A full account of this is given on p.34. We see that Olive eventually succeeded, in piecing together a solution for the care of her children which involved using her neighbourhood contacts for access to information and for practical help; using contacts made through her own ethnic identity for practical assistance; and using her knowledge of local services to get further help from a social worker. It was a difficult time for Olive, but she coped, and showed considerable resourcefulness in the process.

(iii) *Different households do manage their resources very differently, even when they are in apparently similar situations*

These eight households were chosen because of their many similarities, yet one of the strongest impressions of *Eight London Households* is just how very different they all are. In presenting them in her book, Sandra Wallman has put them in pairs which bring out even more similarities: two single parent households; two households of West Indian origin; two 'typical English' households; two households based on second marriages. Yet even within these pairs, the reader is struck by the considerable differences of life style, and in their ways of managing. Wallman does not offer a single explanation of such differences. She argues that they are produced by a combination of factors, of differences in personal and household 'style' which, for example, makes one household welcome changes more readily than another, or which makes one household define its social boundaries and networks more broadly than another's. The Ellisons' social contacts are mostly in the neighbourhood, where they are closely integrated, whereas the Irvings - a household in many respects very similar - have, and make use of, contacts spread widely over much of London, based very largely on the church where the family plays a central role, and reinforced by their ethnic identity.

Contrasts between different households' ways of using available resources can also be seen by comparing the two 'typical English' families - the Bates and the Masons. Both of these families have large numbers of relatives in their network, many of them living quite nearby in south London. Yet there is a major contrast in the way in which these networks are used. Whereas the Bates' keep up very friendly contacts with members of their extended family, they do not expect to turn to them regularly for advice or help, nor do they expect to be used in this way themselves. The Masons have very different relationships with members of their kin group. Here there is a clear expectation that relatives should rely on each other on a regular basis. David and Eileen Mason feel that they give a great deal to their various relatives, particularly in emotional support, often spending many hours just listening to other people's problems. They get a good deal of practical help in return from family members, but it is clear that they find their kin network a drain as well as a resource. They seem to feel that the time spent on helping their relatives could sometimes be used in a better way for the benefit of their own household. The Bates and the Masons seem to have similar resources - a large number of relatives close by but they use those resources very differently. The Masons get more from the network than do the Bates but they do so at a price, which sometimes does not feel worth paying.

Evaluation

The value of *Eight London Households* lies in the insights which it gives into how households actually work, on a daily basis. It shows that households are complex organizations of great variety. People can adapt to their circumstances, and can be very imaginative in working out the best ways to create a good life. The inventiveness of different households in managing their resources can produce notably different ways of life, even where circumstances seem very similar – similar people living in the household, similar houses, similar incomes. So the study shows us that people actively create their own daily lives – life styles are not simply determined by how much money you have, or where you live, or whether you belong to a particular social class.

This study also underlines the importance of thinking about 'households' not simply about 'families'. It is the household – the people who share the same roof – who make up the functioning economic unit. For understanding how resources are managed to support daily life, the fact that they share a household is more important than the fact that members are often also related to each other. In emphasising this, Sandra Wallman is in tune with other sociological work being produced around the same time as her research, for example Pahl (1984) and Brannen and Wilson (1987), who also focussed upon the organization of the household.

Other writers who have assessed Wallman's work have seen it as an important and original contribution. However, some have also criticised her for not pushing the logic of her own approach far enough. Strathern (1986) suggests that the discussion of the ways in which households 'manage' and 'cope' leaves some unanswered questions, especially questions about what managing and coping really mean to the people involved. Would these households really describe themselves as coping, without being prompted? Are they as satisfied with their ability to manage their lives in the inner city, as Wallman implies they are?

Smith (1986) is another commentator who suggests that Wallman did not take her approach far enough. He says that she is right to emphasise that households should be understood within their own locality, but that she should have gathered more data about the local area directly – for example data about the residents association, or about the workplaces of her household members. Without that information, he argues, we only know about the resources available through the eyes of the household members themselves. MacPherson (1985) also wants to know more about the resources available outside the eight households, especially about the use of social security, unemployment services, and other aspects of state welfare, about which the book says little.

It is also possible to criticise this work from the perspective of gender divisions. Though Wallman tells us a good deal about the division of labour between the men and women in her study, she tends to treat resources as available to all members of the household equally. Other research on who has access to 'shared' household resources suggests that (at least in some households) men have a larger share than women – more money at their disposal, the house always heated when they are at home, more and better food (Graham, 1984; Pahl, 1989). This factor is not really visible in *Eight London Households*.

Finally we should note that this research was innovative and unusual in studying eight cases very intensively. In developing this approach, Sandra Wallman drew upon her training in anthropology where the methodology of case studies is well developed (Mitchell, 1983). Of course the research could be criticised as being too small a sample from which to generalise, but this would be unfair, since it does not claim to be a representative study. The purpose was to show the very different ways in which households manage, even when their circumstances seem very similar. This comes through clearly with only eight cases. Possibly more cases would show even more variety.

Conclusion

Official statistics tend to divide households into 'types' (single parents, couples with children, elderly people living alone, and so on). This is obviously useful for some purposes, but one message from Wallman's book is that those uses are likely to be very limited because such data fail to capture the great variety of household experiences in reality, and mislead us into assuming that the quality of people's lives are determined by such characteristics. By looking in detail at how households operate as resource systems, this book reminds us that people are inventive in creating their own daily lives. Even given the same materials, different people will build different lives. These variations cannot easily be captured by talking about different household 'types'. Sociological theories about how families and households work must always take account of that.

Bibliography

Brannen, J. and Wilson, G. (1987), *Give and Take in Families: Studies in Resource Distribution*, London, Allen and Unwin.

Graham, H. (1984), *Women, Health and the Family*, Brighton, Harvester.

MacPherson, S. (1985), Review of 'Eight London Households' in *British Journal of Sociology*, Vol. 36, pp. 635-6.

Mitchell, C. (1983), 'Case and situation analysis' in *Sociology Review*, Vol. 31, No. 2, pp. 184-211.

Morris, L. (1989), *The Workings of the Household*, Cambridge, Polity.

Pahl, J. (1989), *Money and Marriage*, London, Macmillan.

Pahl, R. (1984), *Divisions of Labour*, Oxford, Blackwell.

Smith, G.A.N. (1986), Review of 'Eight London Households' in *British Journal of Social Work*, Vol. 16, pp. 118-9.

Strathern, M. (1986), Review of 'Eight London Households' in *American Ethnologist*, Vol. 13, p. 402.

Wallman, S. Buchanan, I.H., Dhooge, Y., Gershuny, J.I, Kosmin, B. A., and Mann, W. (1982), *Living in South London: Perspectives on Battersea 1871-1981*, London, Gower/London School of Economics.

Appendices

Figure 3.1   Format for network maps.

Map to record geographic distance of people in the household network

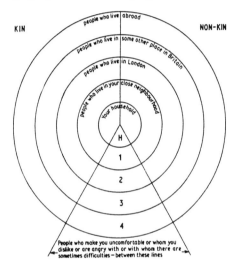

Map to record affective distance of people in the household network

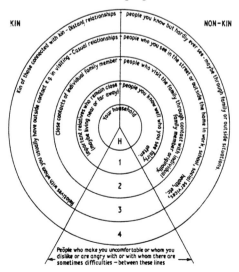

(Wallman, 1984, Figures 4, 5, p.61)

Olive Charles: using resources in a crisis

Sandra Wallman tells this story, partly using Olive's own words (ibid., pp. 103–4):

A crisis came up when Olive was told she must undergo a serious operation. As a single parent her main problem was to find homes for her three children while she was in hospital. For various reasons she 'didn't even consider asking' her relatives living in London. First, they all have large families and full-time jobs, and are 'fully occupied with their own lives'. Second, her two older boys attend local schools and since these relatives live outside the borough, the journey to and from school every day would be long and expensive. Third (an afterthought), Olive is not all that comfortable with them and not keen to ask them any favours. Fourth and most important, she had other options: in previous similar situations one of her local English contacts had looked after the older boys, so she turned to those neighbours to see if they could do the same again. They could not, but after discussion and with their encouragement, another local English contact volunteered to accommodate the older two.

This only left arrangements to be made for the youngest child. He was at that time 18 months old and still demanded a lot of attention. In his case Olive's first choice was one of her 'ethnic' contacts, a close friend from the West Indies, now living in the area. Although this friend worked, she was prepared to make special work arrangements so that she could look after Olive's child. The problem seemed to be solved and Olive was pleased. Then shortly before she had to go into hospital her friend had a crisis of her own and found that she could not keep their arrangement. Olive then went, in some panic, to a succession of other friends, but all of them had work or heavy family commitments. Finally she had no alternative but to contact a social worker. The social worker approached the local community worker for information about possible local foster parents. He recommended a family who turned out to be willing and able to help out by giving the small child a temporary home. In all aspects of this crisis situation, Olive's local contacts were of prime significance as a resource.

4

Family Responsibilities

Janet Finch and Jennifer Mason (1993), *Negotiating Family Responsibilities*, London, Routledge.

Nicholas Abercrombie

Introduction

An important and persistent debate in sociology concerns the notion of family privatization – the idea that families in contemporary Western societies are becoming smaller, more inward-looking, less anchored in traditional kinship relationships and less connected with other related families or the local community. This debate is connected with more public discussions about the alleged decline of family life – of the impact of divorce or the lack of responsibility for caring for relatives for instance. Finch and Mason contribute to this debate by examining family obligations – the sense that one is obliged to provide help and assistance to family members. Such a sense of wider obligation might make families or households less privatized in that they recognize duties to others outside the household.

The Study

Finch and Mason designed a study of these issues in two main parts, a large-scale survey and an in-depth qualitative study. The survey was intended to discover people's *beliefs* about their relationships with their family, not the actual patterns of these relationships. It was based on a sample drawn from the electoral register in Greater Manchester and therefore included a cross-section of people. A total of 978 people were interviewed and this survey population was reasonably representative of the general population. The questions in the survey were organized around a series of vignettes – short stories about various situations in hypothetical families. Respondents were asked what they thought the people in the stories *ought* to do in these circumstances, not what *they* would do. (For an example of a vignette, see p.42).

Clearly the survey was limited in that it could not give data on how beliefs become translated into actual behaviour in families. This was the subject of the qualitative study. Interviewees were drawn from the survey population, and having interviewed them once, some of them were asked for permission to interview their relatives. In this way the qualitative study consisted of eleven kin groups where between three and eight members of the same family were interviewed, and in which 88 people were interviewed, some more than once. This provided a fuller account of negotiations within families from the perspectives of more than one member. It is important to note how these kin groups were arrived at. Essentially, each kin group is the group claimed by an original interviewee who defined who was or was not in it. Other people in this group might not have the same view as to the membership of the group. In the interviews respondents were asked simply to talk about relationships within their own families, concentrating on examples of support and assistance and their sense of responsibility to relatives.

Principal Findings

Family responsibilities

Finch and Mason do not find any very general feeling that the family should be the first port of call for any family member who wants or needs help. For example, in response to the proposition 'Children have no obligation to look after their parents when they are old', 58% of the sample thought there was an obligation and 39% thought that there was not – not a large majority who sense an obligation. There was even less agreement about what kind of help should be given. For instance, in responding to a slightly different vignette concerning responsibilities towards parents who had been injured in a car accident but lived several hundred miles away, 33% suggested a move near the parents, 24% favoured having the parents to live with them, and 25% would offer only financial help. Given this lack of agreement, it seems more appropriate to talk of *guidelines* about family obligations rather than *rules*.

Despite the lack of agreement in principle about precisely what obligations should exist in families, kinship relations remain very important. Almost everyone in the sample had given or received financial help. About half the women – and only slightly fewer of the men – said that they had helped to look after a relative who was ill or otherwise incapacitated. A whole range of other kinds of help is involved as well – practical assistance, looking after children, emotional support. In general, then, the experience of helping, and being helped, is very widespread in families. *Table 4.1*, p.42, shows who gives help to whom. It makes clear that, with the exception of practical support, parent-child support dominates all others.

Reciprocity

The absence of firm rules of family obligation shows the importance of focussing on the *processes* by which decisions are made and carried out. In particular, the study showed that there is a strong moral belief in *reciprocity* – the expectation that, if one gives help, it will be returned at some time. However, Finch and Mason also stress how important it is to understand how reciprocity works in practice. The question of balance is very important. Reciprocal exchanges have to be balanced, and as near equal as possible, so that one party is not permanently indebted to, or dependent on, another.

Sometimes reciprocity can take place by a system of *direct repayment*, in which a service, childcare for example, is repaid directly by the same service. Such exchanges usually take place between members of the same generation. More common, however, is *indirect repayment* where different services are exchanged, child care for assistance with gardening, for instance. The difficulty with indirect exchanges of this kind is fixing on an appropriate rate of exchange – how much child care for how much gardening – which will avoid the possibility of imbalance in the exchange.

Negotiation

The complexity of exchanges, the lack of firm rules, and the difficulty of establishing exchange rates, suggest that a process of *negotiation* must be very important in deciding on family obligations. Families will debate at length on the proper amount of help to be offered and who is going to give it. However, as Finch and Mason point out, negotiations of this kind are frequently implicit and obligations and responsibilities are often allocated without open discussion. However the negotiations are conducted, they take place over time and involve a process of *developing commitments* between particular individuals. There are no fixed rules that determine obligations; rather an individual will take on a responsibility which in turn leads to further responsibilities and the development of a commitment. So, in one of Finch and Mason's examples, an adult son accepted the responsibility of helping his recently widowed mother. Initially, the help took the form of doing some gardening or odd jobs but gradually the scope of the assistance widened and eventually the mother came to live with her son, at which point his wife took on much of the burden of assistance. This process took the form of a negotiation over time which also involved a reciprocity in which the mother helped with household meals.

Finch and Mason distinguish between negotiation by open discussion, clear intention, and non-decision. Open discussions, in which family members get together and discuss what is to be done (the family conference), are very common and some three-quarters of the sample had been involved in such meetings. However, open discussion is also not always negotiation. Certain people may be excluded – often a parent in need of help – and a great deal may be left unsaid which is actually very important to the outcome. Negotiation by clear intention takes place when someone has carefully planned how to give help, and may have implicitly conveyed that intention to others but has not brought it out into the open. Such a strategy may be adopted to give the donor more power; any open discussion might lead to a refusal of help. Quite commonly, this process may go further and the mode of assistance and the person who is to render this assistance are decided without any discussion – there is apparently no decision at all. Indeed, many families take pride in the fact that they do not have to discuss anything – the need to give help is just assumed by everyone.

Legitimate excuses

Family members who do not give assistance usually have to give some account of why they are unavailable to help; they have to give some kind of excuse that everybody will accept as legitimate. In the interview material a whole range of excuses was given for non-involvement. Employment is the most common excuse given particularly where practical help or personal care is at issue. Other family commitments can excuse as well although they can operate in either direction, again illustrating the absence of firm rules in this area. For example, women who have young children can use this as a reason not to help. On the other hand, in some families this can make them *more* available. Many family members may also claim to be incompetent to provide help. Sometimes this may be because of ill-health. At other times it may be because of lack of skill. This last excuse may often be used by men who claim that women are 'naturally' good at personal care and therefore should take the burden of providing it. Commonsensically, geographical distance would seem to be an impediment to active assistance to another family member. To some extent this is confirmed by the study, though again there are no firm rules. On being asked what would be the longest reasonable time for someone to travel one-way each day to care for a sick or elderly relative, 67% of the sample chose under 30 minutes while only 6% thought one hour or over reasonable.

In the process of getting excuses accepted as legitimate, it is also possible that it matters who is asking to be excused. Finch and Mason investigate in particular whether gender or genealogy make any difference. Does it make any difference to the readiness to accept an excuse whether the person offering the excuse is a woman or a daughter? The answer to this is that it does indeed appear to matter. Women on the one hand, and people who are parents or children on the other, are less likely to have their reasons for not helping accepted than men or those outside the parent-child tie. This is often a function of who becomes involved in developing commitments over time. If women are more likely than men to develop commitments to relatives, which is often the case, they are thereby less likely to convince others that they are not able to continue help by virtue of their employment or geographical distance. (For an example of excuses see the Gardners' interview, p.42.)

Moral identities

The negotiations between family members consist of both material and moral exchanges. As will be clear from the discussion of legitimacy, negotiations within families create moral positions – moral identities – for each person involved. Finch and Mason describe this as 'moral baggage' which gets carried forward over time and is reshaped through repeated negotiations.

Central to the construction of moral identities is the idea of reputation and one way of exploring this is to look at how people see the tension between asking for, and offering, help. In general, respondents concluded that asking for help was not wrong in all circumstances. Quite the contrary, it is often entirely right depending on what is asked for and how the asking is done. For example, a loan is more appropriate than a gift. At the same time it is clear from many of the responses that it is not desirable for anyone to be in a position to have to ask, so potential donors have a duty to take the intiative and offer first. This is because, if recipients ask, their <u>moral identities are compromised; they appear dependent or greedy.</u>

These issues are finely balanced as is illustrated in the question of expectation. Respondents were presented with vignettes in which people either expected help or expected recompense of some kind for help given. Generally speaking, expectations of either kind were disapproved of and this probably helps to explain the attitude towards asking. People should not be put in the position of having to ask for help for that implies that they *expect* to receive help. Showing that you expect help and assistance is not acceptable because it suggests that some of the rights of the donor have been taken away. In sum, the ways that people use asking, offering and expecting have to do with keeping the moral identities of *both* giver and receiver intact, particularly the notion that both are independent persons.

Generosity is, in many respects, the mirror image of expectation in that it represents giving that goes well beyond anything that the receiver could reasonably expect. Finch and Mason's interview data contained several examples of behaviour interpreted as generous. In one, a man was given a large sum of money by his wife's parents to buy a partnership in a veterinary practice. On the surface this gift went beyond what the daughter and son-in-law expected. On the other hand, the participants clearly regarded it as entirely appropriate for parents to be this generous to their children and it is this that made it possible to accept the gift. At the same time the recipients had to behave in the right way, that is, they had to show that they did not expect the gift. They defined it as a loan and paid interest on it, despite being told by the parents that this did not matter. If the children had acted in any other way, it would have implied that the gift was not generous. These delicate negotiations protect the moral identities of both sets of parties. The parents can be generous but are acting appropriately as parents; the children construct themselves as independent by not being seen to expect the gift. These then are moral transactions as well as being about the transfer of resources.

Reputations

The way that moral identities are created and sustained in nego-tiations about family obligations is closely linked to the idea of reputation. Finch and Mason make three important claims about reputation. First, there is a shared image of each individual within a kin group. The study was able pick this up because the interviews were done with the relatives of one person. For example, one woman – Mary – gave money to her son when he was out of work. All members of the family portrayed this act of generosity as quite characteristic of Mary. Another of her sons described her in this way:

> 'I thank the Lord for my mum and dad every day. The amount of times that my mum and dad's helped me out, you know. Especially to have someone like my mum to lean on. I don't know how I'd feel – I mean obvi-ously at some time in the future she's going to die. And I don't know how I'll take it.' (Finch and Mason, 1993, p.150)

Reputations are not always this consistent. There may indeed be some-thing of a struggle over reputations with not all family members them-selves recognizing the same reputation.

Second, this image persists over a long time and is difficult to alter. Mary's reputation was well established. Unfavourable reputations will be equally persistent. A son will get defined as someone who is always borrowing money or an uncle is cast in the role of the family black sheep. Such images can even last across generations. Thus a son can almost inherit the reputation, for good or ill, held by his father sug-gesting the speculation that 'some daughters or sons are marked out from childhood, as it were, as the bearers of a particular reputation across generations.' (ibid., p.155)

Third, images are important because they determine how indi-viduals behave towards one another. In particular, reputations provide a structure for negotiations about assistance. People will know who to go to for assistance, who is reliable, and who is good at rendering particular kinds of help.

Evaluation

With studies of everyday life, particularly ethnographies of everyday *family* life, there is a temptation to see the findings as common-sensical; they show us only what we know already. However, what studies of this kind do is lay bare processes that, precisely because they are everyday, we are not formally aware of, even if we recognize them when they are revealed. Futhermore, it is important to note that this particular study does controvert various myths about family obligation. It must moderate extreme accounts of privatization in that Finch and Mason show that many households are involved in a network of help and assistance with other households; they are not purely selfish and inward-looking. At the same time, they also show that the patterns of obligation are very variable. On the whole, there appears not to be a national consensus on what obligations are owed by whom – what children should do for their parents, for example. Furthermore, which family members offer help under what circumstances is highly variable from household to household. This variability has important political implications. Social and welfare policies based on the assumption that assistance of particular kinds is given or should be given by particular individuals (sons or daughters, for example) to their family members (parents, for example) will not command a consensus nor provide a basis for adequate care.

Finch and Mason use an interesting combination of quantitative and qualitative methods. The former relies on strict sampling techniques but informants for the latter were chosen because their kin groups illustrated the kinds of processes in which the authors were interested. The qualitative study was not designed to be representative in any way; one cannot draw inferences from it about the population as a whole. While representativeness is not a main aim of ethnographic studies of this kind, it would have been useful to design the two halves of the study so that they related to one another more closely – to ask similar questions in both halves so that some estimate of the representativeness of the ethnography could be made. Indeed, there are a number of areas in which the choice of families for detailed interviews might well give a misleading impression. For example, families in 'crisis' situations were deliberately excluded. We do not know how common such situations are but the net effect is that we do not learn much about how families manage conflict and struggle. Again, the choice of participant kin groups neglects those individuals who do not participate at all (as distinct from those who offer legitimate excuses) and also those kin groups in which there is relatively little interaction between family members. It should be made clear that these are not situations that the authors wished to investigate; they are, however, certainly ones that deserve investigation.

Conclusion

Finch and Mason's study illustrates the complexity of the debate about privatization. They show that many members of family groups are connected by a web of assistance of many different kinds. This web, however, is not sustained by a rigid set of rules of obligation.

Instead, there are a series of guidelines within which negotiations are conducted. These guidelines concern reciprocity, the balance of independence and dependency, and the importance of protecting the moral identity of giver and receiver. What makes the web of assistance particularly strong, and what counters extreme versions of the privatization thesis, is that exchanges of assistance are as much moral as they are material. They confirm the importance and permanence of family relations and function as a kind of social cement.

Appendices

Table 4.1 Examples of who gives help to whom

	Parents to children	Children to parents	Other
Financial help	89	10	37
Providing a home*	25	18	8
Practical help	10	27	37
Emotional support	35	13	44
Totals	159	68	126

*This excludes 21 young adults who had never left the parental home, but might well do so.
(Finch and Mason, 1993, Table 2.1, p.31)

A Vignette

a. Jane Hill is a young woman with children aged 3 and 5. She was recently divorced. She wants to go back to work and she needs the money. But if she has a job she must find someone to mind the children after school. Her own family live far away but her former mother-in-law Ann Hill, is at home all day and lives nearby. Jane has always got on well with her former mother-in-law.

Should Jane offer to look after Ann's children?
b. Ann *does* offer to help and Jane goes back to work. Some years later Ann has a stroke and needs regular care and help in the home.

Should Jane offer to give up her job and look after her former mother-in-law?
c. Jane *does* give up her job. A year later Jane remarries.

Now that Jane has remarried, should she go on helping her former mother-in-law?

Why do you think she should go on helping/should stop helping? (ibid., p.34)

Example 2: the Gardners

Tim Gardner's account of negotiations about the care of his dying grandfather gives another example of excuses whose legitimacy is disputed. His paternal grandfather had recently been ill, and hospitalised, and this had prompted a set of explicit discussions between Tim's parents, and his aunt and uncle, about where he should live once he was discharged from hospital. In fact, members of neither household wanted Tim's grandfather to move in with them, primarily because Tim's uncle on the one hand, and Tim's mother on the other (that is, his children-in-law) did not get on well with him. Eventually, it was agreed that Tim's parents would take him in, and convert their garage to provide the space to do so, even though Tim's aunt and uncle had plenty of room in their large house. In fact, the issue only ever remained a hypothetical one, because Tim's grandfather died in hospital – but not before certain excuses had been aired.

> *Tim* My auntie and uncle's house, it's turned out since [pause] they've gone on for years saying 'Oh no we're not going to have him.' They used to say this with my gran as well, um when she was like in her wheelchair and so on. The house they've got has got six bedrooms, they had two children who are both now married and moved away. So they're on their own in a six-bedroomed house, but it's, well as my auntie put it, it's not owned by them, it's the company owns it. Well my uncle's a Director of this company and the company bought it for him to live in years and years ago. They said, um, you know 'It's just you and your children, no one else.' So it's all hush-hush and so on from their point of view, so we don't know too much about it. But that seems the basic reason, plus the fact that my uncle *did not* want him in the house. [Emphasis in original]

Tim makes it rather clear that he regards his uncle as offering a flimsy excuse. If his parents, who also 'did not want him in the house', were able to make room for his grandfather, his aunt and uncle could have done something similar, especially since his uncle is a Director of the company which owns their house. Elsewhere his account gives a picture of his parents looking for ways to make it possible for them to provide accommodation and care. He presents them as people who do not avoid responsibilities, and this is rather in contrast with his aunt and uncle whom he views as having developed a history of avoiding responsibilities – first to his grandmother, then to his grandfather. It is this reputation, accumulated over some years, which throws into question the legitimacy of their excuse, and jeopardises 'public' acceptance (that is, acceptance by Tim and his parents) of their claim to be primarily unable rather than unwilling to help. For Tim, their position is not improved by the slightly suspect veil of secrecy drawn over the 'hush-hush' arrangements involving the ownership and use of their house. (ibid., p.114)

5

Mothers and Daughters

Valerie Walkerdine and Helen Lucey (1989), *Democracy in the Kitchen: regulating mothers and socialising daughters*, London, Virago.

Stephanie Lawler

Introduction

Although it is often assumed to be 'natural', mothering is structured by complex social rules. As well as the formal obligations of parents toward their children, which are enshrined in the law and monitored by government social welfare institutions, there exists a range of more informal expectations about what mothering is, by whom it should be done, at what age, and what constitutes 'good' and 'bad' mothering. These expectations, both formal and informal, are subject to wide historical and cross-cultural variation.

Despite increasing mention of 'parenting' in preference to 'mothering', and a theoretical commitment from some fathers to share child-care responsibilities, the work of child-care is still overwhelmingly done by women. This has clear implications for women's participation in other forms of work. Further, because there is frequently an assumption of a natural and straightforward link between giving birth and bringing a child up, child-care is often not recognized as work at all, but is seen as a 'labour of love'.

Democracy in the Kitchen presents an analysis of the relationship between social class and mothering practices. The aim of this analysis is to consider the mother/child pair in the context of their social world, and to analyse the impact of structural inequalities (specifically, gender and class) on their lives. The book also considers how girls of different social classes fare at school.

Democracy in the Kitchen draws on a number of diverse strands in academic work, and makes a contribution to a range of disciplines. It contributes to work on mothering practices, and on the mother–daughter relationship, but it can also be understood within the context of research into women's domestic labour, social class, and education. In addition, it can be seen as contributing to inquiry into the ways in which knowledge is produced, and, relatedly, the links between knowledge-production and practices of regulation. It achieves this by considering the ways in which mothering is subject to a set of knowledge about mothers.

Research Design

Walkerdine and Lucey's study has two principal components. The first is their re-analysis of interview transcripts compiled by social psychologists Barbara Tizard and Martin Hughes for their study of language at home and school (published in 1984 as *Young Children Learning*). Tizard and Hughes's research was based on audio-recordings of 30 four-year-old girls, 15 of whom were from middle-class and 15 from working-class, families. The girls were recorded at home with their mothers and while at nursery school, although the nursery-school transcripts were not re-examined by Walkerdine and Lucey.

The original sample was selected by Tizard and Hughes to consist of two fairly polarized groups. They used the conventional indicator of class – the husband's occupation – in this case using the Registrar General's five main classifications. The middle-class fathers came from RG classes I and II, and the working-class fathers from RG classes III manual, IV and V. In addition, the mother's level of education was taken into account. Only middle-class women who had at least qualified to enter college or university were selected, and only working-class women who had left school at the minimum leaving age with no formal qualifications.

The second component of the research for *Democracy in the Kitchen* is based on interviews conducted by Valerie Walkerdine and Helen Lucey, six years after the original study, with 28 of the girls (two of the middle-class girls were not available to be interviewed). These interviews were concerned with the girls' school careers. The girls, and their teachers, were interviewed, and a standardized maths test was given to all the children in the girls' classes.

In addition to this empirical work, Walkerdine and Lucey examined developmental psychology and educational theory texts, in an attempt to uncover normative assumptions about 'good mothering'. Their analysis throughout the book is presented as a synthesis of this textual and empirical work.

Principal Findings

(i) *The girls at home*

In their re-analysis of the transcripts used by Tizard and Hughes, Walkerdine and Lucey found class differences in mothering practices.

These findings can be broadly divided into two themes: women's work and regulation.

(a) *women's work*

All the girls were demanding of their mothers' time and attention, and those demands often clashed with those of the mothers' domestic work. Walkerdine and Lucey found that middle-class women far more frequently gave in to their daughters' demands. Most of these women involved their daughters in their housework, and structured this work so that it become both play and the basis for learning for their daughters.

Working-class women, by contrast, set up a strong distinction between work and play. They made it clear to their daughters that housework had to be done, usually within a limited time, and, further, that this housework was a priority over 'play'. Although the working-class girls seemed to be more demanding, the tendency of middle-class mothers to give in to their daughters means that it is hard to make any comparison. Working-class mothers more often successfully resisted their daughters' demands.

Walkerdine and Lucey report that, within the middle-class homes, household tasks were never spoken about during the recordings and there was often little indication that they had to be done at all. Working-class women were far more likely to make their housework visible – to talk about it and to make it clear that there were a number of tasks to do in a given period of time.

Walkerdine and Lucey suggest some factors which may have a bearing on the apparent invisibility of domestic labour in middle-class homes. A couple of these mothers employed cleaners and one employed an *au-pair*. Access to a car and enough money to do 'bulk' shopping also makes shopping less time-consuming. But the authors reject these explanations as wholly adequate to explain the 'massive differences' between working-class and middle-class mothers in this area, especially since some studies have shown that the ownership of *labour*-saving devices is not necessarily *time*-saving (see Oakley, 1974, for example). They suggest, rather, that the ways these different groups of women seem to experience their housework has to be seen in the light of their relationship to the paid labour market. In the jobs done by the working-class women (mainly unskilled manual work) it is their time, not their skill, which is bought. There are fixed rules and clear distinctions between 'work' and 'non-work'. Working-class women's lives are structured by these distinctions between 'work' and 'non-work' and it is this knowledge which they pass on to their daughters. Middle-class women trained in professional careers (as most of these middle-class women were), although oppressed by virtue of their gender, own a set of skills which they sell in the job market. They have a different relationship to the world of work: their jobs are more likely to be satisfying in a way that rarely applies to manual labour. Middle- and working-class women, then, attached different *meanings* to the idea of 'work', and this applied also to their housework.

The practice of middle-class mothers of transforming their housework into play for their daughters is the type of mothering practice which Walkerdine and Lucey found to be approved by educational theory. Most of the middle-class women were employed (or had been employed) in the 'caring professions' (social work, nursing and teaching, for example). Walkerdine and Lucey suggest that their training in these professions is likely to have provided them with theories of child development and children's needs:

> So the relationship between work and play and work and time relates to different circumstances of the women, their work, their wealth and poverty, but also to the way in which these things are cross-cut by their understanding and familiarity with modern accounts of child development. (Walkerdine and Lucey, 1989, p.83)

(b) *regulation*

Within the type of analysis used by Walkerdine and Lucey, power is not 'owned' by individuals, as a possession. Power relations are more fluid than this. Mothers, in this analysis, only exercise authority over their daughters by virtue of their role as mothers. Their authority does not *belong* to them. Further, mothers are themselves regulated – either by those government agencies which monitor their mothering or by their own internalization of theories of child development which suggest that mothers must be 'sensitive' to their children's needs. One feature of 'sensitive' mothering, according to Walkerdine and Lucey, is that 'sensitive' mothers must regulate their children without appearing to do so.

All the mothers regulated their daughters through the strategies they used when these girls were demanding, but the middle-class mothers did so in a way which would be deemed 'sensitive' by developmental psychology and educational theory. They were far more likely to tolerate and even to encourage disagreement and challenge from their daughters, to such an extent that these daughters frequently dictated what their mothers would and would not do. This type of mothering practice is usually 'read' as not regulatory at all, but as proof of a state of mutuality and equality between mother and child. Working-class mothers tended to make it clear where the boundaries of good and bad behaviour lay, and to be explicitly in control. They let their daughters know that they could not necessarily have what they wanted, when they wanted it. This type of regulation is usually condemned by child psychology, since it is seen to lead to frustration and apathy in the child. But Walkerdine and Lucey argue that hiding regulation does not make it disappear. They argue that *both* groups of mothers were regulating their children, but in different ways. While working-class mothers generally regulated their daughters by invoking their own authority, middle-class mothers tended to appeal to 'reason'. When daughters' demands or behaviour were seen as out of line, these mothers often told the girls that they were being 'silly'. The point is that the style of regulation used by middle-class mothers is socially approved, while that used by the working-class mothers is condemned.

Theories of child development claim that if sensitive mothers regulate their daughters without appearing to do so, then the child will achieve a sense of her own autonomy. But Walkerdine and Lucey argue that working-class women's relationship to the social order, and the very apparent workings of power and inequality in their lives, may mean that they recognize that they live in an unjust world, in which they are not free and autonomous, and this is what they will pass on to their daughters:

> They know that you cannot have what you want. They do not believe that they are free or have access to plenty. They are poor, often live in bad housing, they work hard, the world is hard. They must teach this to their daughters and they do so often, by making their power visible. They stop, they say no, they regulate overtly. It is a liberal fantasy to believe that power is removed if regulation is made covert, if the girl believes herself . . . to be an agent of free choice, of free will. This autonomy is a sham. (ibid., p.138).

Further, the regulatory strategies used by middle-class mothers – their appeals to 'reason' – were not always effective. The apparent mutuality and equality between mother and daughter was undermined when daughters effectively resisted this form of regulation, for example by blackmailing their mothers (see *Appendices*, p.54). Walkerdine and Lucey found that middle-class women, who were more likely to mother 'sensitively', apparently experienced *more* conflict with their daughters than their working-class counterparts. They report that twice as many middle-class girls expressed direct violence towards their mothers. These girls effectively resisted their mothers' encouragement towards 'reason'. Working-class mothers seemed to accept that there would sometimes be conflict between themselves and their daughters and often created a space in which this conflict could be expressed and rendered harmless (for example in chasing or tickling games).

It is not, Walkerdine and Lucey argue, that working-class mothers and their daughters live in 'an idyll of resolved violence'. But they argue that, while the mother-daughter relationship can be pleasurable and intimate, there will inevitably be times when the daughter feels hostility towards the mother, and even times when the mother feels hostility towards the daughter. Walkerdine and Lucey comment that harmony between mother and daughter is possible, but not all the time.

(ii) *The girls at school*

(a) *achievement at school*

Educational theory proposes a link between 'sensitive' mothering and children's school achievement. The mother is considered to be the child's first teacher, and if she encourages the child's intellectual development by persuading her to reason, and by turning her own housework into educational play, then the child should succeed within the educational system. Walkerdine and Lucey's investigation of the girls' school attainment at the age of ten sets out to examine how far sensitive mothering fulfils this promise.

By ten, the middle- and working-class girls had moved apart in terms of both where they lived and the type of school they attended. At the time of Tizard and Hughes's original study, all the girls were paired so that there was at least one working-class and one middle-class girl at the same nursery school. By the age of ten, only one of the pairs attended the same junior school. The middle-class families had moved to better accommodation and their daughters attended school in these areas. Five of the middle-class girls were at private preparatory schools.

Walkerdine and Lucey report a wide gap between the educational attainment of the middle- and working-class girls at age ten. Some working-class girls were doing very well within their own schools; they evaluated their ability highly, as did their teachers. But their performance was much lower than that of the middle-class girls. The highest attainment was to be found in the private schools and in those state schools in upper middle-class areas which were effectively seen as 'feeder' schools for the nearby public schools.

Two of the working-class girls whose relationships with their mothers were characterized by Tizard and Hughes as most difficult and most fraught were achieving a high standard within their own schools and classes, while the two working-class girls who were considered to have good relationships with their mothers, and whose mothers encouraged them towards reasoning, were failing in comparison with their classmates. On the basis of these findings, Walkerdine and Lucey argue that it is the class structure, rather then mothering practices, which, on the whole, determines whether or not children succeed in education. They comment that only massive changes in the British education system – not prescriptions for good mothering – will enable more working-class girls to 'succeed'.

(b) *teachers' accounts*

Although teachers were not asked for specifically gendered accounts of their pupils, their evaluations of these pupils were highly gender-differentiated. Similar characteristics in boys and girls were interpreted entirely differently by their teachers. Many of the girls of both classes expressed a great many anxieties about school in the interviews. These anxieties were both social and intellectual. Even those middle-class girls whose work was outstanding evaluated their achievement as fairly poor, and these girls often expressed lower self-esteem than their working-class counterparts. However, teachers in both middle-class and working-class schools often denied that the girls were having problems at all and, because they did not recognize the girls' anxieties, they offered them no support. But teachers consistently found anxiety in boys and, further, took it upon themselves to alleviate it. Teachers apparently saw boys and girls differently and provided different levels of support for each gender.

Walkerdine and Lucey argue that the problems experienced by nearly all the girls, in one or another form, are an effect of structural gender inequalities:

> No matter how much their mothers prepared them, this is what the girls have to face. They can manifest the same behaviour as boys until they are blue in the face but this will never 'mean' the same thing. If they are independent they may be a 'madam', if they are strong they may be 'selfish!' (ibid., p.201)

Evaluation

Since *Democracy in the Kitchen* is based on the re-analysis of data, Walkerdine and Lucey did not select the sample group of mothers and daughters, and in fact they express doubts as to the selection process. They suggest, for example, that a woman's social class cannot be adequately measured by her husband's occupation (see Stanworth, 1984).

There are other methodological issues raised by Walkerdine and Lucey's own analysis. The test they administered to the girls and their classmates at age ten (a National Foundation for Education Research standardized mathematics test) is the kind used by local education authorities for selection of children to grammar schools (or their equivalent). Tests such as this are also used as an entry qualification into public schools, and many of the middle-class girls were used to such tests for that very reason. It is by no means clear that the test given is a valid indicator of the girls' overall school achievement, or of their future chances of educational success. This does not undermine Walkerdine and Lucey's overall argument that working-class children, and girls of all classes, are disadvantaged within the educational system (this is well supported by other research).

Tizard and Hughes (1991) express puzzlement over the use made by Walkerdine and Lucey of their research material. They criticize Walkerdine and Lucey's analysis on three grounds. Firstly, they point out that Walkerdine and Lucey are wrong to criticize the original sample for its non-inclusion of Black families, since this was not the case. Secondly, they point out that, in their own analysis of the data, they hardly ever use the phrase 'sensitive mother' and they argue that they did not suggest that sensitive mothering was to be aimed for, nor that middle-class mothers are more likely to mother 'sensitively'. Thirdly, they suggest that Walkerdine and Lucey's analysis is distorted by their self-confessed emotional reaction to the transcript material.

While Walkerdine and Lucey's critique of Tizard and Hughes for their non-inclusion of Black families is clearly factually incorrect, Tizard and Hughes's remaining criticisms raise issues of their own. Walkerdine and Lucey make it clear that *Democracy in the Kitchen* does not represent a specific critique of Tizard and Hughes's work, but of the assumptions of developmental psychology and educational theory in general. They are attempting to uncover some of the implicit assumptions which underwrite Tizard and Hughes's analysis, but the focus of their critique is much wider than this.

Tizard and Hughes's final point rests on an assumption that strong emotions can only distort an appropriate analysis. A number of feminist writers have challenged this view that academic work can only be valid when the observer/analyst is emotionally detached, and indeed they have questioned whether emotional detachment is desirable or even possible.

It does seem that Walkerdine and Lucey are sometimes restricted by their own material. Their suggestions as to why middle- and working-class mothers should regulate their daughters so differently are very convincing. In the absence of interviews with the mothers themselves, they are unable to offer insights into these mothers' own analyses of their motivations. It is always difficult to combine textual and empirical work in this way, since we cannot assume that what individuals actually *do* is necessarily related to what they think they *ought* to do.

Clearly, the size of the sample was relatively small, and would not usually be considered statistically generalizable. However, samples of this size are fairly common in qualitative research of this type, which aims to provide a richness of data and suggestions rather then firm conclusions. It would have been helpful to have had some indication of the questions asked in Walkerdine and Lucey's interviews with the girls at school and with their teachers.

Conclusion

Largely as a result of the impact of feminism on academic research, there is now a large body of literature on mothering and the mother-daughter relationship. This work has been very important in dealing with what was, until recently, a largely neglected subject outside of psychological research. However, as Walkerdine and Lucey themselves point out, much of this work has left intact certain common-sense assumptions of what mothering *is*. The idea that children have a fixed set of 'needs' which is universal and inalienable has often been taken for granted. This means that feminist writing on mothering sometimes reinforces the assumptions which Walkerdine and Lucey are criticising here – for instance that there is a 'right' way to mother, which is somehow outside of social arrangements, or that mothering practices can set daughters on the road to class and/or gender equality.

Democracy in the Kitchen presents an analysis of the mother-child relationship as one which is regulated by State institutions, which themselves draw on the expert knowledges of developmental psychology and educational theory. Walkerdine and Lucey attempt to uncover the assumptions which underwrite these expert knowledges; the assumption, for instance, that certain forms of (hidden) regulation on the part of the mother will erase structural inequalities in the life of the daughter. The point, for the authors, is not to bring working-class mothering 'up to scratch', but to look at why it has been so roundly condemned. In all of these features, *Democracy in the Kitchen* is a highly innovative work.

Walkerdine and Lucey's method of re-analysing Tizard and Hughes's material and reading this material 'against the grain' is interesting and informative. It demonstrates that this type of material is never 'just' data: it relies on interpretation. Even when this interpretation appears neutral, there are always values and assumptions behind it. Of course, this applies equally to Walkerdine and Lucey's own analysis, as they acknowledge. *Democracy in the Kitchen* is a highly political work, and one which challenges the apparent neutrality of much academic research.

Bibliography and Further Reading

Boulton, Maria (1983), *On Being a Mother: A Study of Women with Pre-School Children*, London, Tavistock.

Burman, Erica (1992), 'Feminism and Discourse in Developmental Psychology' in *Feminist Psychology*, Vol.2, No.1, pp.45–59.

Corrigan, Paul (1991), 'Viewpoint: Power/difference' in *Sociological Review*, Vol.39, No.2, pp.309–334.

Ehrenreich, Barbara and English, Deirdre (1979), *For Her Own Good: 150 Years of the Experts Advice to Women*, London, Pluto Press.

Eichenbaum, Louise and Orbach, Susie (1982), *Outside In, Inside Out*, Harmondsworth, Penguin.

Friday, Nancy (1979), *My Mother, My Self: The Daughter's Search for Identity*, London, Fontana.

Nice, Vivienne (1992), *Mothers and Daughters: The Distortion of a Relationship*, Basingstoke, Macmillan.

Oakley, Ann (1974), *Housewife*, Harmondsworth, Penguin.

Phoenix, Ann, Woollett, Anna and Lloyd, Eva (eds.) (1991), *Motherhood: Meanings, Practices and Ideologies*, London, Sage.

Porter, Marilyn (1983), *Home, Work and Class Consciousness*, Manchester, Manchester University Press.

Rich, Adrienne (1986), *Of Woman Born: Motherhood as Experience and Institution* London, Virago.

Riley, Denise (1983), *War in the Nursery*, London, Virago.

Stanworth, Michelle (1984), 'Women and Class Analysis: A Reply to John Goldthorpe,' in *Sociology*, Vol.18, pp.159–170.

Tizard, Barbara and Hughes, Martin (1984), *Young Children Learning*, London, Fontana.

Tizard, Barbara and Hughes, Martin (1991), 'Reflections on *Young Children Learning*' in G. Walford, (ed.), *Doing Educational Research*, London, Routledge.

Urwin, Cathy (1985), 'Constructing Motherhood: The Persuasion of Normal Development' in Steedman C., Urwin, C., and Walkerdine, V. (eds.), *Language, Gender and Childhood*, London, Routledge and Kegan Paul.

Appendices

Regulation and work:

[C. = child, M. = mother]

Emily (a middle-class girl) and her mother:
C: Shall we play – Mummy, I want you to play this game with me.
M: All right . . . No, shall we, shall we start our lunch and play it afterwards? Do you think?
C: No . . . Orange, blue, yellow, green, red. (C. has already got the game out and is pointing to different-coloured clowns on the box.)
M: Shall we do our lunch and then do it afterwards?
C: No.
M: I think it's going to take us rather a long time, that game.
C: No! (screams)
(Walkerdine and Lucey, 1989, pp.77–8)

Nicky (a working-class girl) and her mother:
C: Mum, will you come upstairs and play.
M: Nicky, I'm sorry, I cannot come up yet.
C: Oh you said when . . .
M: I'm just going to do this work first, love. I've got washing to do.
C: Yeah?
M: Got ironing to do.
C: Yeah?
M: I got altering to do.
C: Yeah?
M: Yeah, well it all takes time, love.
(ibid., p.81)

Blackmailing the mother:

Angela (a middle-class girl) is playing with a box of Vim. Her mother has explained to her that it is dangerous, and that, if Angela agrees not to eat it, she will let her go on playing with it:

M: It's not good for you, you can pretend . . . you'll have to pretend but you mustn't put it in your mouth . . . you won't, will you?

C: No . . . but it, I will if you, if you don't get a, a, a saucer for my dolly (Angela gets the saucer, which her mother had previously denied to her)

(ibid., p.113)

Violence:

Liz (a middle-class girl) and her mother:

C: Don't whistle, if I hear you whistle again I'll smack your bottom!

M: No, you won't.

C. Whistle again then. Whistle again!

(M. Whistles and C. hits her on the back)

M: Don't, Liz. I'm harder than you so I should be very careful.

C: I'm going to be harder than you.

M: Quite frankly, I'm not interested in that game at all. It's rather silly.

C: I'm going to poke you in the eye one day.

M: You'd better not. That's a very unpleasant thing to say, why d'you say that?

C: 'Cos . . . you're being naughty.

M: No I'm not. What have I done wrong?

C: You . . . I don't want you to whistle.

M: You're just being silly.

(ibid., p.123)

Jacky (a working-class girl) and her mother. Jacky pretends to hit her mother who then pretends to hit her back:

C: You can't even touch me. You can't do it. (Laughs)

M: You didn't even touch me.

C: I did. Did! (Laughing)

M: That doesn't hurt. Doesn't hurt.

C: Look! (C. really hits M.)

M: Next time you do it I'll smack you.

C: I 'macked you!

M: No, *I'll* smack *you*.

C: (Laughs.) You didn't know what to do, what to do.

(ibid., p.131)

Table 5.1 Educational achievement

Rank order of school means (p = private)		
Test scores	Middle class	Working class
124.80	Emily (p)	
119.08	Samantha (p)	
117.34	Helen	
116.25	Naomi	
115.91	Charlotte (p)	
112.44	Gill	
112.24	Penny	
112.15	Liz	
111.50	Amanda (p)	
108.36		Jacky
108.12		Jenny
106.65		Maureen
106.65		Teresa
104.70		Nicky
104.11		Susan & Katy
102.08	Diana	
101.97	Angela	
101.37		Anna
98.85	Julie	Patsy
96.64		Kerry
94.87		Dawn
92.15		Sally

(ibid., p.191)

These are the average scores for each of the girls' school classes, not the scores of the girls themselves. Only 24 of the girls are included, because two of the middle-class girls were not available to be tested, and there were four occasions when, because of lack of time, the classes could not be given a standardized test.

6

The Family Meal

Nickie Charles and Marion Kerr (1988), *Women Food and Families*, Manchester, Manchester University Press.

Alan Warde

The Sociology of Food

Food is a central social fact. A decent diet is a major precondition of good health. Eating is an emotionally highly-charged activity, as everything, from people's fondness for their own mother's cooking to illnesses like anorexia, indicates. Food takes up a significant proportion of most households' budget – 19% on average in 1988 – and shortage of proper food is one of the most cruel deprivations associated with poverty. Moreover, its preparation takes up a lot of women's time, for women are overwhelmingly the providers. Food habits tell a great deal about the texture of family relations, the generation and reinforcement of gender divisions in the household, and social distinctions between people belonging to different social categories.

Women Food and Families reports on food preparation and consumption in households in northern England. It considers the divisions of labour between men and women in shopping and cooking, their different tastes, the amount of food they and their children consume, the use of food in everyday life, in family celebrations and in entertaining. These processes are examined to throw light on health and diet, social customs, gender divisions and family organization.

Despite the fact that food habits provide an arena in which to examine many vital social processes, they have rarely been investigated by sociologists. Charles and Kerr provide the only systematic recent empirical investigation of British food practices. Their work can, however, be understood in the context of many other studies of social relations within families and households. In particular their work fits into a tradition of inquiry into *domestic divisions of labour* and *gender relations within the family*.

Research Design

In their research Charles and Kerr collected data from 200 women, each of whom had at least one pre-school child. They were, therefore, relatively young. They lived in and around York in northern England and were interviewed in 1982/3. Of the sample, 119 (60%) were not in employment, and of the remainder most were in part-time, rather than full-time, work. Ten lived alone with their children and six had unemployed husbands. The sample had a class distribution not much different from the national average.

Data collection involved two interviews with each woman, a fortnight apart. During that fortnight, the woman kept a diary recording what every household member ate and drank. The interviews covered a wide range of topics, likes and dislikes, family routines, special occasions, dieting and so forth. Responses were transcribed and coded for a computer so that the data could be analysed numerically, to discover, for instance, what proportion of men cooked meals and what amounts of food different individuals ate. The interviews included many open-ended questions and verbatim responses generated valuable qualitative data as women discussed the meaning of cooking, family meals and nutrition. The women were allowed to talk in their own language so that their understandings could be documented. This complemented the statistical data and helped in its interpretation.

Principal Findings

The study concentrated on three main issues: (i) the meaning of food within families and its role in family relationships; (ii) class differences; and (iii) gender divisions of labour.

(i) *Food patterns and meanings*

The main motif of Charles and Kerr's research was the continued central importance to the British family of 'the proper meal'; hot meat (or sometimes fish) and two vegetables. Main meals did not always consist of meat and two veg, but that was the ideal and alternatives, like vegetarianism, were restricted to a tiny minority of middle class households. Moreover:

> . . . a proper meal is defined not only by its contents but by the way it is eaten and what happens during the meal in terms of behaviour. It is also defined by who is present. It is ideally a meal which is a "family" meal and this, by definition, requires all members of the family to be present. It is also a meal cooked by the woman in the household for herself, her partner and her children. Thus if her partner is away at the time of the main meal when a "proper" family meal is normally cooked and eaten it has an effect on the content of the meal. Of the women's partners, 132 had been absent from the main meal at some time or another and 47% of these women ate differently when their partners were away, 31% ate at a different time and 14% ate in a different place. (Charles and Kerr, 1988, pp.21–2)

In the minds of respondents there is a link between the proper meal and the proper family, eating together being one symbol of familial harmony. In addition, around the family meal, children, besides learning table manners and food tastes, were socialised into appropriate gendered behaviour.

Charles and Kerr demonstrate, through quotations from their interviewees, the emotional significance of food. Food is used to placate and to punish children; to keep husbands happy and faithful and prevent them going back to mum; and to discipline the body, through dieting. Consequently women often feel guilt if proper food is not provided or if their children eat too little. One respondent said about preparing food for her little daughter:

> I used to get very uptight because if I'd cooked something I thought was nice and would do her a lot of good and she just wouldn't touch it. It's an emotional thing . . . Because you feed your family that's one way of expressing love . . . and I realised I did get upset and of course she cottonned on – she's very bright – that was the way to really get me going. (ibid., p.92)

Equally women feel upset if they themselves eat too much: the tyranny of the ideology of body shape and its complicated relationship to self-image is brought out in the account given in the *Appendices, Passage 6.1,* p.64. Food consumption is laden with social meaning.

(ii) *Class differences*

Charles and Kerr succeed in showing some variation by class in meal patterns: the middle class more often eat at table, less often watch television while eating, and more frequently talk to one another during meals. Some of this difference is due to cramped conditions among poorer households, but that is insufficient to explain the differences in style. Quality of foodstuffs varies too, as do shopping habits and the factors involved in deciding what to buy; the middle class giving more consideration to health, working class women showing more concern with price. Patterns of entertaining also vary by class, especially what sort of people will be entertained (whether kin or friends and colleagues), what degree of effort is likely to be expended, and whether alcohol is served. This is consistent with evidence about class differences in friendship and leisure (see Allan, 1979).

Few people eat proper meals all the time. At minor meals middle class households are more flexible in what they will eat. This is partly a function of income, but also of cultural preference. The Registrar General's classes I/II (professional and managerial) are rather more adventurous, more conscious of nutritional guide-lines, and more likely to use health foods, fresh vegetables, fruit, raw food, cheese, pasta and pulses (see *Table 6.1,* p.63). Charles and Kerr observe that the working class maintains the same structure to its non-primary as to its main meals (for example, sausages, beans and chips is basically meat and two vegetables cooked differently). Middle class households, by contrast, will accept bread, omelette and salad as a meal.

There have been many disputes about how to measure class (see Charles, 1990). Charles and Kerr took note of the occupational class of men and women separately. They found that as regards food *taste*, the woman's previous occupation was more important statistically than her partner's present job in explaining variation (see *Table 6.1*). On the other hand, the participation of men in cooking and shopping is more determined by male class position (see *Table 6.2*, p.64). While *Table 6.2* does indicate class differences in behaviour, these might be thought relatively weak compared with differences between men and women.

(iii) *Gender and the domestic division of labour*

The extent to which men and women share domestic tasks is significant for several reasons. Sociologists have considered the domestic division of labour indicative of different kinds of marriage relation, as a distinctive type of work and as an index of social inequality between men and women (see Warde and Hetherington, 1993). Recently there has been extensive debate about whether men are increasing their participation in housework; this might be expected since married women are increasingly likely to be in paid employment outside the home and because sharing fairly has become contentious. Much domestic labour goes into providing meals; food has to be bought, cooked, served and cleared up afterwards. *Women Food and Families* contributes to the accumulating evidence.

Charles and Kerr found that women do most of the physical and mental work involved in food preparation. The research showed that there were very sharp differences in the amount of labour done by men and women in the kitchen. Women did almost all the work. Only 25 men cooked on a regular basis and only two (unemployed) fully shared cooking. Shopping was shared more; but even then in only 24 households did the man do half or more. Moreover, even when men are involved, it tends to be as helpers, rather than by taking responsibility for organizing tasks. Women do the planning and the vast majority of the work.

Despite the fact that women did the food preparation, many aspects of the activity were determined by men. Unsurprisingly the routines associated with husbands' employment have a constraining effect on the organization of mealtimes, but in addition their tastes are given preference. Charles and Kerr conclude that:

> Women cook to please men, they decide what to buy in the light of men's preferences, they carry the burden of shopping for food and cooking food, but most of them carry out tasks within a set of social relations which denies them power, particularly when they are at home all day with young children and are dependent for financial support on a man. (ibid., p.40)

The predominance of men's preferences is apparent from *Passage 6.2*, p.64, which is one of several recorded illustrating how women sub-ordinate their own tastes to those of men. Only 25 women (about 8% of those living with a partner) said that they would continue with the same eating habits if 'they were living on their own' (ibid., pp.73–4). What would most likely be abandoned would be some meat dishes and the routine of proper meals.

Food preparation also entails caring work. As we saw above, emotions of love, discontent and conciliation are expressed through food. The symbolic significance is demonstrated by the possibility of resistance. That refusal to eat with the family, among adolescents, or refusing to eat a dish that has been cooked for dinner (more common among husbands), are deemed to express rejection merely indicates the investment of emotion and caring that is embodied in food. Women almost exclusively provide such care.

Critical Observations

Until recently there has been little other sociological research on food (for a survey of literature on the sociology of food see Mennell *et al.*, 1992). The phenomenon of the proper meal had been detected earlier by Murcott (1983) in South Wales; official reports had pointed to differences in class tastes; and attention had been drawn to the gender divisions of domestic labour in studies from the mid 1950s onwards (compare Oakley, 1974; Willmott and Young, 1973). There is thus little empirical basis for challenging Charles and Kerr's findings. While predominantly receiving praise for its unique and detailed study of routine food production, it gave rise to some reservations among its reviewers.

One concern was the degree to which evidence from their sample can be generalized. Beardsworth and Keil (1990, p.142) and Prout (1991, p.404) argued that, because all the women in the sample had a pre-school aged child, domestic processes associated with one particular stage of the life-course would be exaggerated. This is the stage of the life-cycle where women do the greatest share of tasks, for when engaged in paid work, especially full-time paid work, their share of domestic work falls. Similarly, as regards the pattern of food consumption, once there are teenagers around, regular family meals become less frequent.

Secondly, Woodman (1989) expressed doubt about taking the women respondents' answers about their partners' and children's behaviour as faithful descriptions of what actually happens. Certainly, the level of conservatism or conventionality displayed by the sample, both in terms of domestic divisions of labour and food taste attributed to other household members, was relatively surprising for a cross-sample of British people.

Third, both Woodman and Popay (1990) were concerned that Charles and Kerr, while describing class differences among the women, failed adequately to explain them. Charles and Kerr used the Registrar General's classification of occupations, though that is rarely most appropriate for sociological purposes. They presented evidence using 'both women's and men's occupational class, usually selecting for presentation the one which shows the clearest correlation' (ibid., p.9). They thereby demonstrate class differences, though arguably not especially strong ones, in aspects of food practice. By contrast, other recent studies of domestic divisions of labour have usually concluded that class differences are of relatively minor significance (e.g. Pahl, 1984). Because most of these households were heavily dependent on a single (mostly male) wage, the effect of income might be confused with that of class (for they are strongly associated). In a sample of households further advanced in the life-course a woman's labour market position (whether full-time, part-time or homemaker) might become a stronger predictor than class.

Conclusion

Women Food and Families provides systematic information about an important, but neglected, area of everyday life. In this account, the central food patterns of the UK remain very conservative (though they have changed in some respects since the 1950s, with more varied foods available, less regular meal times, fewer people taking breakfast, etc.). This may partly be the result of the particular sample in which, for instance, households were in the earliest stages of married life with small children and 'ethnic minorities were virtually unrepresented' (ibid., p.8). There is little evidence of any profound change in domestic divisions of labour, women continuing to play a subordinate and servicing role in the household and to perform tasks traditionally ascribed to them. Notwithstanding some quibbles about the measurement of class position, the research also indicates the persistence of social class in determining aspects of household practice and cultural reproduction.

Bibliography and Further Reading

Allan, G. (1979), *The Sociology of Friendship and Kinship*, London, Allen and Unwin.

Beardsworth, A. and Keil, T. (1990), 'Putting the menu on the agenda: a review article' in *Sociology*, Vol.24, No.1, pp.139–152.

Charles, N. (1990), 'Women and class – a problematic relationship' in *Sociological Review*, Vol.38, No.1, pp.43–89.

Charles, N. and Kerr, M. (1988), *Women Food and Families*, Manchester, Manchester University Press.

De Vault, M. (1991), *Feeding the Family: the social organisation of caring as gendered work*, Chicago, Chicago University Press.

Mennell, S., Murcott, A. and van Otterloo, A. (1992), *The Sociology of Food: eating, diet and culture*, London, Sage.

Murcott, A. (1982), 'On the social significance of the "cooked dinner" in South Wales' in *Social Science Information*, Vol.21, Nos.4/5, pp.677–95.

Oakley, A. (1974), *The Sociology of Housework*, London, Martin Robertson.

Pahl, R. (1984), *Divisions of Labour*, Oxford, Blackwell.

Popay, J. (1990), Review of 'Women Food and Families' in *Journal of Social Policy*, Vol.19, No.3, pp.431–3.

Prout, A. (1991), Review of 'Women Food and Families' in *Sociological Review*, Vol.39, pp.403–5.

Warde, A. and Hetherington, K. (1993), 'A changing domestic division of labour?: issues of measurement and interpretation' in *Work Employment and Society*, Vol.7, No.1, pp.23–45.

Woodman, D. (1989), Review of 'Women Food and Families', in *Sociology of Health and Illness*, Vol.11, pp.196–7.

Young, M. and Willmott, P. (1973), *The Symmetrical Family: a study of work and leisure in the London region*, Harmondsworth, Penguin.

Appendices

Table 6.1 Average number of times specific foods eaten during diary fortnight by occupational class (defined according to the woman's current or last full-time occupation; figures in brackets represent class patterns of consumption defined by men's occupation)

		Women	Men	Children
High status meat:	I/II	4.2 (4.4)	4.4 (4.4)	3.1 (3.1)
	IIIN	4.5 (4.4)	4.9 (4.9)	3.1 (3.0)
	IIIM	4.7 (4.7)	5.5 (5.1)	3.2 (3.2)
	IV/V	4.4 (4.3)	4.7 (4.3)	2.8 (3.0)
Chips:	I/II	2.9 (3.4)	1.7 (1.4)	2.9 (2.8)
	IIIN	4.7 (4.2)	5.4 (5.6)	4.2 (3.8)
	IIIM	5.3 (4.7)	6.2 (5.7)	4.3 (4.5)
	IV/V	5.7 (5.3)	5.7 (5.5)	5.4 (4.6)
Fresh fruit:	I/II	10.0 (9.1)	7.9 (7.0)	11.8 (11.1)
	IIIN	5.6 (4.5)	4.6 (5.1)	6.6 (5.8)
	IIIM	4.1 (4.3)	4.8 (3.9)	5.9 (5.5)
	IV/V	3.6 (4.3)	2.0 (4.8)	3.5 (5.4)
Milk:	I/II	9.2 (9.1)	8.9 (9.0)	22.6 (24.1)
	IIIN	5.6 (4.8)	5.9 (6.1)	22.4 (19.6)
	IIIM	4.1 (4.8)	4.9 (4.7)	20.5 (21.4)
	IV/V	3.6 (4.1)	4.3 (4.3)	17.2 (19.3)
Alcohol:	I/II	3.9 (3.8)	5.4 (5.8)	0.2 (0.2)
	IIIN	2.7 (3.2)	4.3 (5.3)	0.2 (0.3)
	IIIM	1.2 (2.5)	3.1 (3.6)	0.1 (0.1)
	IV/V	2.4 (1.0)	2.6 (1.5)	0.3 (0.0)

(Charles and Kerr, 1988, compiled from Tables 9.1, 9.2, 9.3 and 9.6, pp.194–202)

Table 6.2 Responsibility for meal preparation by social class of male partner

	I/II	IIIN	IIIM	IV/V	Student	No partner	Total
Self prepares all meals	32 (53.3)	16 (57.1)	52 (66.7)	13 (61.9)	1 (50)	6 (60)	120 (60.3)
Self mainly, partner sometimes	24 (40.0)	9 (32.1)	16 (20.5)	7 (33.3)	—	—	56 (28.1)
Either or both (50/50)	—	—	1 (1.3)	1 (4.8)	—	—	2 (1.0)
Self mainly with help from partner and/or children sometimes	—	3 (10.7)	6 (7.7)	—	—	2 (20)	11 (5.5)
Other	4 (6.7)	—	3 (3.8)	—	1 (50)	2 (20)	10 (5.0)
Total	60 (100.0)	28 (100.0)	78 (100.0)	21 (100.0)	2 (100)	10 (100)	199 (100.0)

(ibid., Table 8.4, p.177)

Passage 6.1: Woman talking about ambivalent attitudes to food and body weight (ibid., p.142)

'It's a vicious circle. If I feel I'm overweight I get upset so I eat 'cos I hate being overweight, it really upsets me. I hate it. It's all tied in with my having a baby as well because – because I've had a baby I don't want to look frumpy or old so obviously it's important to have a nice figure so that you are not going to look old and horrible and everything, but because I'm slightly overweight I eat then to comfort myself. I mean, even though I am sat here telling you this and I know I do it but after all I can't stop myself doing it. I still do it and then I feel terrible afterwards. After I've done it, you know, I'll have a mad binge, and then I feel so utterly desolate after I've finished, I think "you stupid fool". Then I go and do the same thing the next day because I think, "Well I've already done it the day before so I'm off my diet anyway". It's stupid . . . [laughs] I know it's there but I can't stop it [. . .] Perhaps I'm mad.'

Passage 6.2: Wife reporting on husband who only liked plain food (ibid., p.72)

'If I cook something that's got a whiff of herbs in it or something he'll put his knife and fork down and say, "I'm sorry but I'm not eating it." Occasionally he'll get through it but I have known him to refuse to eat it and maybe go and have a biscuit or a piece of cake instead. [Interviewer: How do you feel about that?] Not very happy. He usually waits until my parents come and I've prepared something a bit out of the ordinary and he'll leave it. I'm not happy but there again I'll not make a scene. I'm not one for rowing – I'll go off and have a little weep to myself. It's all over. I mean we never argue much about anything like that and then he'll probably say sorry and eat it next time but the next time I know better and don't put it in.'

7

When Husbands Stay at Home

Jane Wheelock (1990), *Husbands at Home*, London, Routledge.

Andrew Sayer

In the traditional domestic division of labour, the male 'breadwinner' left all, or most, of the housework to his wife. This arrangement tends to hold where married women are in employment too, so that in addition to their paid work, wives work a 'second shift' at home. In many areas, the decline of traditional male occupations and the consequent rise in male unemployment have dealt a blow to the traditional set-up. Meanwhile female employment has remained relatively bouyant.

In such cases one might expect to see a role reversal, with wives as breadwinners and their partners as househusbands. However, in most cases where husbands become unemployed, their wives also give up their jobs (Morris, 1985, 1987). This is not only a result of men's resistance to their wives taking on the role of breadwinner. It is also an effect of low pay and the rules governing welfare benefits; women's earnings are unlikely to be higher than state benefits and the latter are in any case reduced in proportion to their earnings. So there is little economic incentive for women to become the breadwinner. Nevertheless, in some cases, women married to unemployed men do keep up their paid work. This raises the question of what happens then to the division of domestic labour. Who does the housework?

Husbands at Home is a study of 30 families in which the husband was unemployed and the wife was employed at least part-time. All of them live in Wearside in north east England, where male manual employment has collapsed while female employment has risen. The book analyses the domestic response to these labour market conditions, looking at how housework is divided up within the family and how much it has changed from when the husband was employed. In addition it analyses the couples' attitudes to their domestic arrangements. The presentation of this empirical work is preceded by chapters on the theory of labour market change and its relationship to the domestic division of labour.

Analyses of the domestic division of labour and *gender relations* have become popular in sociology, countering the traditional identification of 'work' with employment (Oakley, 1974, 1981; Pahl, 1984; Yeandle, 1984; Hetherington and Warde, 1993). Most studies have focussed on households in which men – and often women – have been in employment. There has been some research on unemployed households (e.g. Morris, 1987), but this has concerned families in which women as well as men are unemployed. The results of these studies have not shown much difference from the traditional domestic division of labour. One would expect the traditional arrangement to be most under pressure where husbands are unemployed while their wives are still employed, and this is the distinctive focus of Wheelock's research. Such households are unusual, but they are especially interesting for assessing the strength of the traditional domestic division of labour.

Research Design

Wheelock selected her 30 couples from a random 10% sample of working class areas of Wearside. The criteria for selection were: (i) the husband should be unemployed; (ii) the wife should be employed; and (iii) there should be children under the age of 16. The reason for the inclusion of the third criterion was to ensure that the domestic workload would be heavy. In fact, couples meeting all three criteria were so rare that some households with adult children living at home had to be included to make up the 30. The men were all formerly employed in traditional manufacturing industries such as shipbuilding and mining. The women were currently all in low paid manual jobs (e.g. cleaner, home help, factory operative). Clearly, having to live on low wages and state benefits meant that the couples did not have the option of buying in domestic assistance.

The primary source of information was semi-structured interviews held jointly with husband and wife. These lasted one to one and a half hours and gave sufficient information to enable the author to interpret individual behaviour in its particular context. Data were gathered on who did three major tasks (main meal, washing and ironing) and two minor tasks (hoovering and washing up). The three major tasks tend to be more strongly identified as women's work than the minor tasks. Using these data, an index was constructed to measure the degree of husbands' involvement in housework. This was then used as a basis for classifying the households. The interviews also provided qualitative information on the tasks and on attitudes to housework.

It is important to realise that this is an *unusual* set of families, for as we have already noted, in most families in which married women go out to work their husbands are also employed. When men lose their jobs, their wives also tend to become unemployed. Wheelock quotes the following figures from the *General Household Survey* of 1985 on two-parent household employment structure: 37% of women married to employed men were unemployed or 'economically inactive'. ('Economically inactive' means not actively seeking paid work. Of course, what the term conceals is the fact that the women are very active in the *domestic* economy!); 78% of women married to *unemployed* men in Britain were unemployed or 'economically inactive'. Thus, while 62% of women married to employed men were working in the labour market, only 22% of women married to unemployed or economically inactive men were themselves in employment.

Principal Findings

The study focussed on two main issues: (i) the nature of the division of housework between husband and wife, in the context of the latter's paid work commitments; and (ii) the couples' attitudes to housework.

(i) *The domestic division of labour*

The most important finding was that, although the women still had primary responsibility for a core of household tasks, the husbands had become more involved in housework than hitherto, albeit to varying degrees. Their contributions ranged from occasional help with a few minor tasks to routine work on bigger tasks such as ironing and meal preparation. Some of the men used their time for themselves rather than for doing housework – birdwatching, going to the club, fiddling with the car – or only did housework or childcare when it fitted in with such activities.

It is not just the number of domestic tasks undertaken that matters, but how much effort is put into the task and the degree of responsibility taken for its planning. 'Childcare' might involve just being in the house with children or, alternatively, feeding them and changing and bathing baby. There is a big difference between deciding what shopping is needed and doing the shopping. Generally, the men's involvement in, and responsibility for, the tasks that they actually did was limited compared to that of their wives. It is significant that 'bottoming' – the most *thorough* kind of cleaning involving moving furniture – remained the women's preserve. Even where the husbands did the cleaning as part of their weekly routine their wives would 'bottom' at weekends.

There was a clear relation between the number of hours of paid work done by the wives and their husbands' contribution to housework, the latter being greatest where their wives were in full-time employment (see *Table 7.1*, p.72).

As the table shows, nearly a quarter of the families retained a 'traditional rigid' division of labour, with men doing little beyond traditional men's tasks like DIY and car maintenance. The women in these households worked from 4 to 16 hours per week.

> The Briggs . . . are a family of four children; the oldest daughter aged 19 in full-time employment, an unemployed son, and 12 year-old twin sons. Mr Briggs was a red leader in the shipyards until he had been made redundant . . . He had always prepared the vegetables for Sunday lunch and put the meat in the oven . . . He had also always shared doing the decorating, but this was the limit of his domestic contribution . . . Mrs Briggs took a day-time cleaning job, working twelve and a half hours a week . . . The eldest daughter also helped her mother with making the main meal . . . When asked whether there had been any differences in what he did in the house Mr Briggs said "I cannot think of any". Mrs Briggs agreed . . . "We just went on the same, just went on regardless" . . . The changes for Mr Briggs are that he is "free all day, just lounging about, tinkering with the car". (Wheelock, 1990, pp.91–2)

A slightly larger group were classified as 'traditional flexible'. The husbands in these families took on a few minor tasks such as washing up and helping with shopping.

Eight families were classified as 'sharing' households. As Wheelock points out, this does not involve anything approaching 50–50 equality, but rather a situation where the husband takes on jobs such as hoovering, shopping and cooking on a systematic basis, and takes some responsibility for their planning. The women in this group were employed for 12 to 30 hours per week.

Finally, in the 'exchanged roles' category (seven families), the husbands had more substantial responsibility for housework, though even here the traditional roles were not fully reversed, for the women still did jobs such as washing or 'bottoming'. The wives in this group worked from 15 to 40 hours per week. Perhaps surprisingly, there were more dependent children amongst the exchange-role families than the sharing and traditional flexible families. Possibly this indicates that the cost of supporting such families encouraged the wives to change to a breadwinning role while the volume of domestic work forced the husband to undertake it.

The Sterling family were the most extreme example of an exchanged roles household:

> . . . (They) have three sons aged nine, eight, and five. Mr Sterling has not worked since he lost his job as a labourer five and a half years ago . . . (U)ntil she took a full-time job as a machinist one and a quarter years ago . . . "he never thought of doing a thing". But when they were both at home, Mr Sterling suffered from boredom: "I didn't have anything to do when we were both in the house" . . . (Since Mrs Sterling returned to work) Mr Sterling has . . . been virtually in charge of all the housework and childcare during the week . . . (he) plans and makes the main meal, but Mrs Sterling gets the shopping in on Friday afternoons since she finishes work early that day. She also hoovers right around and does the washing – "She'll not let us do that" says Mr Sterling – on Saturday.

(ii) *Attitudes*

Only a few of the men showed any sign of thinking that gender roles in the household should be changed as a matter of principle. The main reasons they gave for doing housework were overwhelmingly prag-matic – boredom, filling in time. Only one man saw advantages in his wife being the sole breadwinner, the others wanted to be back in paid work. Work was a source of male companionship and identity, ' "(Being unemployed) takes you out of the manly role. I used to be the bread-winner with my meal on the table. It lowers you. I feel like a lodger in my own house." ' (husband in 'traditional rigid' family (ibid., p.63))

Differences between attitudes and actions were common; some individuals had radical attitudes that weren't reflected in practice, others – the 'reluctant flexible' and the 'reluctant sharing' couples – retained beliefs in more traditional arrangements and resented having to break with them. According to Wheelock, in these latter cases, it was the *wives* who were the more attached to the traditional roles. However, the most striking case of ambivalent attitudes was that of the husband who did the most work in the sample. On the one hand he said: ' "I cannot expect the wife to come in and do (the housework) after a full day's work . . . I'm in the house all day and I'm not going to sit on top of muck, I'm not going to neglect me bairns" '. On the other, he also felt that ' "it should be the bloke out working and the women in the house." ' (ibid., p.96)

Many of the women regarded the quality of the housework done by men as inferior, whether because their husbands lacked the skills or the inclination, or because their standards of cleanliness were lower. There were disagreements over what housework needed to be done, with the women demanding higher standards than the men and, as in the case of bottoming, having to do the jobs themselves to get those standards. ' "To me I like to do the jobs when I'm ready to do them and in the way I want them done; since he's in the house all day he's doing it. I won't interfere . . . but it doesn't get done the way I wanted it done." ' (ibid., p.125)

Although many of the women were reluctant to change traditional domestic roles, their attitudes to their paid work were far from negative: all expressed commitment to their work, describing their jobs 'in considerable detail, and with obvious enthusiasm' (ibid., p.146), despite the low pay and low status of their jobs. This commitment was further demonstrated in practice by the very fact that they continued to go out to work for little or no financial gain. In ten of the cases the financial benefits were minimal or even negative. In six of these families, the husbands were in receipt of supplementary benefit from the state. Any earnings over four pounds that the women made were deducted pound for pound from their husbands benefit. In addition to this, levels of pay in the jobs which the women did were so low as to make it difficult for them to earn enough to do without welfare benefits. There was therefore a formidable 'poverty trap' or 'unemploy-ment trap', discouraging women from being the sole earner. The 30 couples selected for study were therefore unusual in disregarding these economic constraints. Patriarchy, the system of state benefits and low pay all combine to deter women from employment, and yet the women in the survey were resisting these pressures. Ironically they were doing so even though their attitudes towards the domestic division of labour were conventional.

This is one of the most interesting findings of the research. Wheelock argues that it shows that self-respect can override narrow considerations of economic rationality. A purely material explanation of human needs is clearly inadequate. Paid work was not regarded negatively as a sacrifice but positively as a source of identity and self-respect. Moreover, contrary to views of the poor as 'scroungers', the families were trying to reduce or avoid dependence on the welfare state – even though the benefit system actually *discouraged* them from working.

Critical Observations

Husbands at Home was generally welcomed as a novel contribution to research on the domestic division of labour, focussing on a particularly interesting set of households. It established that there was some change from the traditional model, more than registered in earlier research. However, the reviewers found Wheelock's conclusion that this amounted to a significant change in men's involvement somewhat optimistic, for as the results indicate, only a minority changed much and many hardly changed at all. Moreover, even some of those who moved away from the traditional model did so reluctantly, and there was little enthusiasm for changed roles amongst the wives. The author's view that 'feminists . . . may see hope for a less gender segregated future arising from the changing behaviour of this group' (ibid., p.152) therefore seems unconvincing.

Here, and on a few other occasions, Wheelock tries to make generalisations about the implications for domestic labour amongst *all* families, overlooking the special nature of the survey couples and the fact that many of the individuals had changed under duress rather than willingly. This raises the interesting question of whether the domestic divisions of labour of such couples would become more traditional again if the men found jobs or if the women gave up their's.

One reviewer noted that eleven of the men were on invalidity benefit, and suggested that more account should have been taken of the effects of their situation on their outlook and behaviour (Millar, 1991).Possibly it might have been easier for them to rationalise their domestic role than those who had no disabilities.

Wheelock describes the domestic arrangements as 'strategies', 'negotiated' by those involved. But these terms could be misleading, implying a greater degree of planning and more equality between husband and wife than actually exists. The inequalities in work loads and responsibilities could be interpreted as implying unequal power and lack of negotiation.

Reviewers found the book's observations regarding the wives' motivation to do paid work for minimal economic reward particularly interesting. But as Millar notes, if going out to work helped the women to retain their self-respect, it is a pity that Wheelock did not say more about how the men maintained their's: they did not seem to gain much self-respect from housework.

It would be interesting to find out more about why women did not appear to favour non-traditional arrangements. Is it because they felt – with some justification – that men couldn't or wouldn't do domestic jobs properly? Or because they felt uneasy about expressing feminist beliefs in the presence of their husbands? Or because they had been socialized into traditional views on gender roles and hadn't yet changed them to bring them into line with their current circumstances?

It would also be interesting to compare more affluent households in this situation, including ones in which women have a stronger position in the labour market, to see if their responses and attitudes were different.

Conclusions

Wheelock's research deals with a minority group of households, though one which is especially interesting from the point of view of the domestic division of labour, since the pressure on men to do housework is particularly strong. It shows households responding to a combination of difficult labour market conditions, patriarchal values and practices, and the state welfare system, and in ways that might not have been predicted. *Husbands at Home* represents an interesting case study, not only for the changes in behaviour it reveals but for the complex attitudes and motivations associated with them.

Bibliography and Further Reading

Blake Turner, J. (1992), Review of 'Husbands at Home' in *Contemporary Sociology*, Vol.21, No.2, pp.247–9.

Devine, F. (1991), Review of 'Husbands at Home' in *Sociology*, Vol.25, No.1, pp.176–7.

Millar, J. (1991), Review of 'Husbands at Home' in *Work, Employment and Society*, Vol.5, pp.476–8.

Morris, L. (1985), 'Renegotiation of the domestic division of labour in the context of redundancy', in Roberts, B., Finnegan, R. and Gallie, D. (eds.), *New Approaches to Economic Life*, Manchester, Manchester University Press.

Morris, L. (1987), 'Constraints on gender: the family wage, social security and the labour market' in *Work, Employment and Society*, Vol.1, No.1.

Oakley, A. (1974), *The Sociology of Housework*, London, Martin Robertson.

Oakley, A. (1981), *Subject Women*, Oxford, Martin Robertson.

Pahl, R.E. (1984), *Divisions of Labour*, Oxford, Blackwell.

Warde, A. and Hetherington, K. (1993), 'A changing domestic division of labour?: issues of measurement and interpretation' in *Work, Employment and Society*, Vol.7, No.1, pp.23–46.

Yeandle, S. (1984), *Women's Working Lives*, London, Tavistock.

Appendix

Table 7.1 Re-articulation of the Divisions of Labour: classification of the sample families

Classification	Name of family	'Bottoming', 'emergency', or 'large family factor'	Hours of employment for wife	5-task grading	Age of youngest child	No. of families	% of families
Exchange	Bradshaw	B	FT	+0.5	Secondary		
Roles	Kelly	B	32	+0.5	Primary		
	Mawson	B	32	+1	Adult		
	Sterling	B	FT	+1	Primary	7	23
	Toward	B	FT	+1	Primary		
	Turner	B	FT	0	Secondary		
Partial Exchange	Johnson	E, LF	15	+0.5	Primary		
Sharing	Archer		$12\frac{1}{2}$	0	Secondary		
	Kidd		20	+1	Secondary		
	Kirby		20	+1	Adult		
	Harris	E	18	+0.5	Adult	8	27
	Laws	B	$22\frac{1}{2}$	+0.5	Adult		
	Smart	B	$29\frac{1}{4}$	+1	Adult		
Reluctant	Giles	B	20	0	Adult		
Sharing	White	B	20[1]				
Traditional	Bewick		$22\frac{1}{4}$	+0.5	Adult		
Flexible	Carrick		18	−0.5	Adult		
	Crowther		$25\frac{1}{2}$	−0.5	Adult		
	Hogg	E	$7\frac{1}{2}$	0	Adult	8	27
	O'Brien		20	−0.5	Adult		
	Potts		$4\frac{1}{2}$	0	Adult		
Reluctant	Bolam	B	$17\frac{1}{2}$	−0.5	Primary		
Flexible	Dennis	B	FT	+0.5	Adult		
Traditional	Briggs	LF	$12\frac{1}{2}$[2]	−1	Secondary		
Rigid	Brown	E	5[3]	−1	Adult		
	Coulthard	E	4	−1	Adult		
	Milne	LF	16	−0.5	Preschool	7	23
	Moody	E	14[4]	−1	Adult		
	Tennet*		$12\frac{1}{2}$	−0.5	Primary		
	Ward[5]		mornings	n.a.	Secondary		

Notes:

[1] Mrs White gave up her job in July 1985.

[2] Mrs Briggs gave up her job in June 1985.

[3] Mrs Brown worked 16 hours a week until February 1985.

[4] Mrs Moody took up her second job of 10 hours a week in January 1986.

[5] This is a classification based on the limited information from the doorstep interview.

* This family is traditional flexible for childcare.

(Wheelock, 1990, Table 4.3, p. 114).

8

Television and Family Relationships

David Morley (1986), *Family Television: Cultural Power and Domestic Leisure*, London, Comedia.

Alistair Billam

The Family and the Television

Most people watch television everyday. We do not merely watch television, we talk about it, and sometimes even to it! Television is a global phenomenon. People from different cultures the world over watch television – in many cases, the same programmes. Despite the pervasiveness of television in peoples lives, it is often regarded, by both academic and common sense opinion, as a threat to the moral fibre of the individual or to society as a whole. According to such views, we are all seen as passive receptacles of the 'plug-in drug' which extinguishes our critical faculties in the malaise of constant television viewing. However, even though many people hold this common sense view, people continue wanting to own more television sets and consume their programmes with increased vigour. (By 1991, 99% of all British households either owned or rented one or more television sets and watched for an average of 26 hours a week (*Social Trends*, No. 23, 1993).

Most television viewing occurs within the home. It is therefore an activity primarily associated with the family. Indeed, it is feasible to regard the television set as 'one of the family', for it is welcomed into the home, given a central position in the main living room and, increasingly, situated in most other rooms in the house as well. As a consequence of the pervasivness of television within family life, the ways in which television viewing is organized, and the habits that arise as a consequence of viewing, tell us much about the social relations within the family.

Family Television reports on television consumption in households. Central questions are 'who decides which programme(s) to watch' and 'who acquires strategic use of television technology' (the video-cassette recorder, the remote control, etc.). In addition, *Family Television* explores 'television related talk', the amount, type and level of commitment involved when watching television, and programme and channel preferences. These areas are examined to shed light on gender divisions, family organization, the social uses of television, and the ways in which individual choices and reactions to television are situated in, and affected by, social and cultural contexts.

Morley's work was one of the first and most influential studies of the domestic use of television. However, the study is an extension of several sociological lines of enquiry, most notably, *gender relations within the family, reception analysis, audience ethnographies*, and more generally, *cultural studies*.

Research Design

Morley's research was based on data collected from 18 families in south London during the Spring of 1985. The families consisted of two adults living together with two or more children up to the age of 18. All the families were white and all possessed a video-cassette recorder. Morley does not state exactly how the sample was selected. As *Table 8.1*, p.82 shows, the sample was manual-working class/lower-middle class biased (as a consequence of its geographical location). Families where the head of the household belonged to classification groups B and C1 were of the 'builders made good' sort, and not professionally educated. Neither did they command high levels of *cultural capital*, although some of the respondents did earn relatively high incomes. The head of the household in five of the families was unemployed (see *Table 8.1*). The sample is not therefore, representative of wider society. As a consequence, the results of the study should not be generalised to the viewing habits of the British population as a whole.

The data were collected by in-depth interviews lasting between one and two hours. The two adults were interviewed together in the first part of the interview, then an offer was extended to the children, if they wished to participate. The interviewing method used by Morley was 'unstructured discussion'. This means that no interview schedule was used, and the respondents were able, at least to some extent, to dictate the direction of the interview. This method can be contrasted with 'structured interviews', which tend to place more importance on the reliability of the questions.

Morley argues that the method of unstructured discussion allowed him to differentiate between responses resulting from the stereotyped roles inevitably assumed by members of families, and those which were more 'real'. Therefore:

> . . . the interviewing method was designed to allow a fair degree of probing. Thus on points of significance I returned the discussion to the same theme at different stages in the interview, from different angles. This means that anyone 'putting me on' (consciously or unconsciously) by representing themselves through an artificial/stereotyped *persona*

which has no bearing on their 'real' activities would have to be able to sustain their adopted *persona* through what could be seen as quite a complex form of interrogation! (Morley, 1986, p.52)

The qualitative approach that Morley took was, therefore, *ethnographic*. That is, the researcher immersed himself as fully as possible within the social activities of the respondents, which were manifest during the discussions, and kept careful notes about his observations on these activities. The interviews were recorded and transcribed for ease of analysis and interpretation.

Principal Findings

The study concentrates on the central issue of gender. According to Morley, men and women regard their time at home in different ways. For men, the home is a site of leisure, seen as something distinct from 'industrial time', a retreat from the public (work), into the private (home/leisure). For women, however, the home is a site of work. Whether they have work outside of the home or not seems to have little influence here, for the responsibility for domestic chores remains that of the women. This observation forms the basic starting point for the analysis of the interviews. It underlines the fact that men are more able to spend more time watching television, and with a more whole-hearted concentration. Women, from necessity, tend to watch television in a more distracted, guilty, and less free manner. The study highlights many effects of gender relations within the household, five of which are examined below.

(i) *Programme preferences*

The study indicated that a sharp distinction exists between the programme preferences of men and women. The former tend to prefer 'factual' programmes such as news, documentaries and current affairs, whilst the latter indicated a preference for fictional programmes. A good example is given by *Family 6* of the study:

F6 Man: 'I like all documentaries . . . I like watching stuff like that . . . I can watch fiction but I am not a great lover of it.'
F6 Woman: 'He don't like a lot of serials.'
F6 Man: 'It's not my type of stuff. I do like the news, current affairs, all that type of stuff.'
F6 Woman: 'Me and the girls love our serials.'
F6 Man: 'I watch the news all the time, I like the news, current affairs and all that.'
F6 Women: 'I don't like it so much.'
F6 Man: 'I watch the news every time, 5.40pm, 6pm, 9pm, 10pm, I try to watch.'
F6 Woman: 'I just watch the main news so I know what's going on. Once is enough. Then I'm not interested in it.'

(ibid., p.82)

Even within fiction programmes themselves, there was a distinction between the 'realist' (close resemblence to 'real' social life) fiction, preferred by men, and the 'romantic' fiction preferred by women.

(ii) *Power and control over programme choice*

The study found that when a conflict arose over programme choice, it was usually resolved in favour of the male. Masculine power is thus the ultimate determinant, and is even more so, Morley argues, when the television includes a remote control handset. Some of the women in the sample complained of their partner's 'channel hopping' when they were trying to watch a programme. The remote control facility was often perceived by members of the families as the father's symbolic possession, and to be used almost exclusively by him. The exceptions to this were found in the families with unemployed fathers. In these families it was usual for the father to record his preferred programmes to be watched later, either when the rest of the family had gone to bed or the following day when they had gone to work and school. Morley argues that this factor is particularly interesting because it highlights the negotiated nature of relations within the family. For example, the male has not usurped power within the family as a consequence of some biological determinant. He does not have the symbolic possession of the remote control as a result of being a 'man'. Instead, power in the family is socially arrived at. The role of the male in the household, and the degree of power he holds depends on a social definition of what constitutes 'masculinity'. Therefore, 'masculinity' is seen as being intertwined with the male's economic activity (his occupation), and notions of the 'breadwinner'. Morley argues that when this socially constructed role of masculinity is undermined and deemed problematic, for example when the man becomes unemployed and the woman is working, masculine power becomes less rigid and more negotiable. As a consequence, the man may find it increasingly difficult to determine the family's television viewing, because he is no longer conforming to a socially arrived at definition of the masculine role.

(iii) *Styles of viewing and television related talk*

The study points to distinct ways in which men and women watch television. Men tend toward a style (or mode) of viewing which allows them to watch attentively, preferably in silence and without interruption. Futhermore, the men in the study often found it hard to understand their wives' and daughters' style of viewing. For women tend to see the act of watching television as a social activity. That is, it involves conversation, and quite possibly, at least one other simultaneous domestic task, such as ironing. For the women in the study, to watch television in the male style – watching television and doing nothing else – would be a 'waste of time'. Furthermore, the women often mentioned that their husbands would 'go on at them to shut up', whilst the men often mentioned how they could not understand how their wives and daughters could follow programmes if they were doing something else.

The following extracts from some of the study's respondents illustrate this well:

> F5 Man: 'It really amazes me that this lot [his wife and daughters] can talk and do things and still pick up what's going on. To my mind it's not very good if you can do that.'
> F5 Woman: 'Because we have it on all the time it's like second nature. We watch, and chat at the same time.'
>
> (ibid., p.131)
>
> F18 Woman: 'I knit because I think I am wasting my time just watching. I know what's going on, so I only have to glance up. I always knit when I watch.'
>
> (ibid., p.151)
>
> F15 Woman: 'I can generally sit and read a book and watch a film at the same time and keep the gist of it. If it's a good film it doesn't bother me. I'm generally sewing or something like that.'
>
> (ibid., pp.132/3)
>
> F9 Man: 'I like to watch it without aggravation. I'd rather watch on my own. If it's something I just want to watch. I like to watch everything with no talking at all.'
> F9 Woman: 'Every now and again he says, "Ssshh shut up". It's terrible. He comes in . . . from a pool match and he'll say. "Shut up, please shut up!"'
>
> (ibid., p.156)

Generally, the study found that women were more likely than men to talk about what they see on television (particularly fictional programmes) to friends, relatives and workmates. Men implied that to admit doing this (particularly about fictional programmes) would in some way underml_ine their masculinity. The exception to this was sport, which men did admit to talking about. So, even though men watch television more attentively than women, they are less likely to talk about it to their friends. To some extent, this discrepancy can be explained by the fact that the cultural role of femininity is more expressive than the masculine one. However, as Morley points out, the study is primarily concerned with the respondents' accounts of their behaviour. Therefore we are only presented with a picture of what the respondents *admit* to being their behaviour.

> F6 Woman: 'I go round my mate's and she'll say, "Did you watch *Coronation Street* last night? What about so and so?" And we'll sit there discussing it. I think most women and most young girls do. We always sit down and it's "Do you think she's right last night, what she's done?" Or, "I wouldn't have done that," or "Wasn't she a cow to him?" . . . Then we sort of fantasise between us, then when I see her the next day she'll say, "You were right," or "See, I told you so."'
>
> (ibid., p.134)
>
> F18 Man: 'I won't talk about television at work unless there'd been something like boxing on. I wouldn't talk about *Coronation Street . . .*'
>
> (ibid., p.160)

(iv) *Technology: use of the video*

Just as the remote control handset was used primarily by the man, so the video recorder was seen largely as the property of the man or his sons. Women rarely used them, relying on their husbands or children to work the controls for them. Possibly as a consequence, the women had little power and influence over choice of rented video films, and rarely visited video rental libraries. In addition, when family members had their own tape for recording, it was often the case that the women would allow their tapes to be used by others whose tapes were full.

The alienation that women experience in relation to the video recorder can, according to Morley, be seen in terms of gender expectations. For example, even though women are used to working sophisticated forms of domestic technology, the place of women within the social relations of the family pushes women into being technologically incompetent in relation to the video recorder. Such a level of incompetence falls neatly, argues Morley, into the 'classic' mode of 'dependent femininity' which 'needs' masculine 'help'. As one woman respondent said: 'I can't use the video. I tried to tape *Widows* for him and I done it wrong. He went barmy. I don't know what went wrong . . . I always ask him to do it for me because I can't. I always do it wrong. I've never bothered with it.'

(v) *Solo viewing, guilty pleasures and masculine hegemony*

The tendency for women to watch television inattentively is overruled when they view, in the words of one of Morley's respondents, 'a nice weepie', or one of their favourite programmes when the rest of the family are not around (hence 'solo' viewing). It is only when the rest of the family are absent, and thus their domestic responsibilities alleviated, that they feel free enough to participate in the viewing style associated with husbands. For the women in the study, the attentive mode of viewing is seen as an indulgence, something which they can only participate in when other members of the family are absent. They see this as the only time when television can be watched attentively without having to 'keep an eye' on the needs of others.

The study found that some women would record a specific programme and later invite friends around to view it together, usually in the afternoon when the other members of the family were out. For example:

> F5 Woman: 'That's one thing we don't have on when he's here, we don't have the games programmes on because he hates them. If we women are here on our own – I love it. I think they're lovely . . . If I'm here alone, I try to get something a bit mushy and then I sit here and have a cry, if I'm here on my own. It's not often, but I enjoy that.'
>
> (ibid., p.135)

Morley argues that many women accept what he terms a 'masculine hegemony', which involves their acceptance of their programme preferences as 'silly', 'inconsequential' and 'trivial'. Thus, not only do men see their wives' programme preferences as low in status, but the women themselves see their preferences in this light as well.

It is from this premise that Morley was able to identify the 'guilty' pleasures some women associate with television viewing. Women's 'solo viewing' is often infused with 'guilt'. Once the masculine hegemony is accepted, 'they (the women) then find it hard to argue for their preferences in a conflict because, by definition, what their husbands want to watch is more prestigious. They then deal with this by watching their programmes, when possible, on their own, or only with their women friends' (ibid., pp.161–2).

Women's television viewing is 'guilty' because it occurs within a masculine hegemony which has been internalised by women. By devaluing women's television tastes, men are, in effect, devaluing them socially. One woman talked about the 'guilt' of television viewing:

> F17 'When the children go to bed he has the ultimate choice. I feel guilty if I push for what I want to see because he and the boys want to see the same thing, rather than what a mere woman would want to watch . . . if there was a love film on, I'd be happy to see it but they wouldn't. It's like when you go to pick up a video, instead of getting a nice sloppy love story, I think I can't get that because of the others. I'd feel guilty watching it – because I think I'm getting my pleasure whilst the others aren't getting any pleasure, because they're not interested.'
>
> (ibid., p.162)

Evaluation

Television, and the media in general, have, for some time, been a major source of interest to sociologists. The social uses of the television, and the ways in which the television fits into domestic and family relations are, however more recent topics of inquiry. Subsequent ethnographic research of television audiences has in many ways echoed Morley's overall standpoint (see, for example, Lull, 1990), or has built on, rather than refuted, the study's principal findings. Nonetheless, there have been a series of criticisms levelled at the study, though most of these are anticipated by Morley within the text.

Firstly, there is the problem of the representativness of the sample. Lull (1987) points out that the small size of the sample would have been less of a problem if Morley had concentrated on the *microscopic* details of television viewing. But Morley attempts more than this, by implying that some of the processes he identifies are generalizable to groups outside of his sample. Thus when Morley speaks of 'significant' numbers of women in his study making a particular point, it must be remembered that at most, this was only 18 women. As a consequence, it is problematic to extrapolate from such comments.

Secondly, the study is less a book about 'Family Television' than a study of 'gendered' television! There are two related points here. First,

Lull (1987) points out that the children who were supposed to be a central aspect of the study are rarely mentioned. If the child respondents had been included within the research in a more systematic way, the study's conclusions may not have been so overtly concerned with male/female relationships but, instead, have given an account of *family* relationships. As Morley argues in the afterword to *Family Television*, the original intention of the research was to interview the whole family together. However, he found that in practice such interviews were 'impossible' to conduct, especially with young children who quickly got bored with the interview arrangement. Second, Hermes (1991) argues that by concentrating on the gender/power relations within the family, Morley overlooks the 'particularities of everyday life' and loses sight of everyday interaction. Morley is accused of dogmatically looking for (and finding) gender relationships to the exclusion of all other daily routines which make up social life. In addition, Ang and Hermes (1991) argue that the role of gender should not, *a priori*, be seen as a 'basic determining factor' of television consumption. They argue that Morley too readily accepts the inevitability of gender as a determining factor of media consumption practices. Gender *may* be a determining factor of consumption practices, but it does not necessarily have to be one.

A third major criticism is that Morley fails to give adequate analysis of the influence of factors other than gender, such as age and, in particular, class.

Lastly, Acland (1989) and Peters (1987) argue that the political edge of Morley's earlier work (e.g. *The Nationwide Audience* (1980) which addressed differential 'readings' by members of different occupational and class groupings to the same 'Nationwide' television programme) has been blunted by a concern with domestic relations. Both maintain that *Family Television* is in some way superficial because it does not address the content of television and thus ignores questions related to the role of ideology. This position has been termed 'the retreat into the living room', and refers to a trend within media sociology to address the uses media are put to by audiences, rather than to examine the potential effects of their ideological content on audiences.

Conclusion

Family Television is an important contribution to the growing body of research on audiences. It provides complex and detailed analysis of what is, to most people, a common everyday occurrence; watching television. The study highlights the extent to which gender relations are crucial in understanding the role of the television in family life. Such evidence is in keeping with the notion that domestic divisions of labour have remained largely unchanged in recent years, and that (despite methodological problems, which prevented the study from examining other influential factors) unequal relationships between men and women remain of central concern for sociologists.

Bibliography and Further Reading

Acland, C. (1989), Review of 'Family Television' in *Journal of Film and Video*, Vol.41, No.3.

Ang, I. and Hermes, J. (1991), 'Gender and/in media consumption', in Curran, J. and Gurevitch, M. (eds.), *Mass Media and Society*, London, Edward Arnold.

Hermes, J. (1991), 'Media, meaning and everyday life', paper presented to International Television Studies Conference, London, July 1991.

Lull, J. (1987), 'A First of its Kind – Review of Family Television', *Journal of Communication*, Vol.37, pp.124–127.

Lull, J. (1990), *Inside Family Viewing*, London, Routledge.

Morley, D. (1980), *The 'Nationwide' Audience*, London, British Film Institute.

Morley, D. (1986), *Family Television: Cultural Power and Domestic Leisure*, London, Comedia/Routledge.

Morley, D. (1992), *Television, Audiences and Cultural Studies*, London, Routledge.

Peters, M. (1987), Review of 'Family Television' in *Initiatives* (SEFT), April 1987.

Appendix

Table 8.1 Sample details

	Family	Family Income	Job (Head of Household)	Age left Education (HoH)	Home Status	Years in Residence	Holidays in last year	Political Preference	Approximate age of youngest child
	F16	£11k	Builder (S-E)	19 years	Owner	$8\frac{1}{2}$	1	Con	6
	F11	£12k	Manager	18 years	Owner	10	1	Lab	6
B	F8	£15.5k	Carpenter/Builder (S-E)	15 years	Owner	18	1	Con	12
	F4	(?)	Furniture Dealer	19 years	Owner	10	1	?	18
	F9	£16.5k	Salesman (S-E)	15 years	Owner	11	1	Lab	12
C1	F14	£11.5+	Caretaker	16 years	Owner	$1\frac{1}{4}$	1	Con	6
	F15	£17k	Decorator (S-E)	16 years	Tenant	$1\frac{1}{2}$	2	Lab	6
	F17	£12k	Fitter	17 years	Tenant	10	1	Lab	12
	F13	£12k+	Caretaker	15 years	Tenant	10	3	Lab	12
C2	F18	£7.5k+	Builder (S-E)	15 years	Tenant	3	2	Con	18
	F12	£13k	B Telecom Technician	15 years	Owner	20	2	?	18
	F10	£10k	Postman	17 years	Tenant	2	3	Lab	6
	F7	£8k	Service Engineer	14 years	Owner	28	6	Lab	12
	F6	u	Ex-builder	16 years	Tenant	13	0	Lab	18
	F5	u	Ex-ambulance worker	14 years	Tenant	17	1	Con	18
U	F3	u	Ex-landscape gardener	15 years	Tenant	7	0	Lab	6
	F2	u	Ex-decorator	15 years	Tenant	5	1	Ecol	18
	F1	u	Ex-caretaker	16 years	Tenant	$\frac{1}{4}$	0	Lab	6

Notes:
[1] The class categorisations have been made by means of what is, in the end, an intuitive judgement, whereby class is assessed as a factor of incomplete education background × cultural capital × home status. A simple income calculation would produce a different categorisation. I am using the standard ABC, etc., classifications merely as a descriptive short-hand to give a rough indication of class position.
[2] The sample is, unfortunately, rather restricted at the top end of the scale. It lacks any substantial representation of the higher educated, professional classes.

(ibid., p. 54)

9

The Social Transition from School

Michael Banks, Inge Bates, Glynis Breakwell, John Bynner, Nicholas Emler, Lynn Jamieson and Kenneth Roberts (1992), *Careers and Identities*, Milton Keynes, Open University Press.

Alan Warde

Background

Compulsory schooling ends at 16 years of age in England and Wales, at 15+ in Scotland. Almost all young people must then decide between continuing education, a job or training. The decision is fateful. It has a major impact on long-term life chances as well as leading to rather different short-term experiences for young people choosing alternative routes. The post-16 move constitutes a key social transition, significantly determining occupational, domestic and political 'careers'.

The transition from youth to adulthood is accomplished by ritual celebration in many societies, but it is a somewhat hazy boundary in contemporary Britain. Here it can involve several events including entering the labour market, becoming financially independent, leaving the family home, establishing long term relationships and parenthood. The order in which these occur, and the speed of change, varies considerably from case to case and is often protracted over many years. The final outcomes or destinations are also very different. In the process an adult identity and a fresh set of responsibilities are assumed.

Intellectual Context

Studies of the transition from school to work address a range of topics of general sociological interest. They throw light on adolescence and youth culture, for this is a stage in the life-course said to involve the stabilisation of concepts of self, increasing independence from parents, development of personal and sexual relationships, enhancement of gender identities, and the formation of political consciousness. These processes always occur in, and are shaped by, a particular economic and political environment. In the 1980s, industrial restructuring produced very high levels of unemployment with considerable differences between local labour markets, such that job opportunities varied from place to place. Also, this was a period of acute political reform by the 'Radical Right' governments of Mrs Thatcher. Policies were introduced to alter education and training, employment conditions and social security provision. It was also intended that general social values should change to enhance respect for enterprise, personal independence and market transactions. Such economic and political changes structure social inequality. Transitions from school display and entrench class, gender and regional differences in economic opportunities and personal social development.

Sociologists have often used the term 'career' to describe the passage of individuals, over time, through a patterned series of situations. 'Moral', 'patient' and 'deviant' careers are familiar sociological concepts, though 'occupational' career remains the most common. Banks *et al.*, in *Careers and Identity*, talk of several sorts of career – economic, social, personal and political. They examined the stages that young people in the mid-1980s typically passed through between the ages of 16 and 20. The most common five routes at age 16 were as shown in *Figure 9.1*, p.91. At the end of compulsory schooling the options were: continuing a full-time academic course; a full-time vocational course; entering employment immediately; going via the Youth Training Scheme (YTS) into employment; or becoming unemployed.

The investigators sought to explain what determined young people's decisions. They also inquired whether these career choices affected personal relationships, social activities and political attitudes.

Methods

The study covered four areas in Great Britain: Swindon, Liverpool, Sheffield and Kirkcaldy. Several teams of researchers were involved. They used an integrated mixture of survey, interview and ethnographic methods of data collection. Two 'cohorts' of young people, selected from school records, completed questionnaires in each place in 1987. The older cohort was aged 17 or 18; the younger was in the last year of compulsory education, aged either 15 or 16. There were about 600 youths in each cohort in each place. Every respondent was asked to fill in another questionnaire in 1988 and 1989. (There were inevitably some problems in tracing the same people at the later dates.) In addition, a sub-sample, picked to represent the different vocational routes post-16, was chosen for structured interviews (110 in each town) on two other occasions. These forms of data collection produced quantitative evidence which was analysed statistically. Other techniques were also used. Ethnographic methods were used to analyse the different learning experiences of trainees and students on YTS, BTec and A-level schemes in Sheffield. In Kirkcaldy, nine individuals were interviewed in-depth, on a number of occasions, as were their parents, in order to explore in more detail how transitions were experienced by individuals.

Principal Findings

(i) *Determinants of career routes*

The proportions of young people aged between 16 and 18 passing along the different routes from compulsory schooling are broken down by area, gender, cohort, educational attainment and social class background in *Table 9.1*. Careers are affected by the local area in which students live. Thus 29% of all school leavers went straight into employment in Swindon. In the other three areas, the proportion was between 8% and 11%. This reflects the nature of local labour markets. Swindon, relatively prosperous and in the south of England, had many more job opportunities. By contrast, over a third of people in the North and Scotland passed through YTS into unemployment (i.e. they had not held a job for more than six months since leaving school). Gender differences were comparatively slight, girls being marginally more likely to continue in full-time education. Little difference was apparent between the two cohorts, though the younger group was more likely to remain in education. Unsurprisingly, those with the best educational qualifications at age 16 were the most likely to remain in the educational channels. Conversely, those with the poorest qualifications were very much more likely to find themselves facing YTS and unemployment. Class background was also strongly associated with post-school careers; the higher the social class, the more likely was continued education and *vice versa*.

Experience between 16 and 18 affected subsequent progress. *Table 9.2*, p.92 shows what happened to young people pursuing different channels in the subsequent two years. Those who took the A-level route were very likely to continue into higher education and very unlikely to become unemployed. Those who had obtained a job sometime between 16 and 18 were very likely to keep it thereafter: thus 88% of those who had obtained a job straight from school, and also 88% of those who had acquired a job after YTS training, were still employed at age 20. The group without employment between 16 and 18 had much the highest continuing rates of unemployment, though two thirds had obtained jobs by the time they reached 20 years of age. The harrowing and disruptive experience of long-term unemployment for young people, which is more prevalent in the early 1990s than in the late 1980s, is documented in other recent studies (see Coffield, 1986; Allatt and Yeandle, 1992).

The authors' analysis suggests that the critical decisions about career paths have already been made some time before pupils sit their GCSE or Scottish Ordinary examinations. Those who decide to leave tend to have a higher commitment to work than those who remain in education – a process of 'anticipatory socialization' occurs. The benefits of an income and the status of being in work are highly prized by many young people and those successful in obtaining work at 16 express considerable satisfaction. Indeed, a high level of commitment to employment is widespread; only a quarter of respondents in 1987 disagreed with the statement that 'having almost any job is better than being unemployed'.

(ii) *Social class and career*

Systematic and repeated observation of the behaviour of groups on YTS, BTec and A-level courses in Sheffield suggested that courses recruited from different class backgrounds and that the social relations between teachers and students varied accordingly. The young men on a YTS bricklaying scheme behaved on their day in college in exactly the same marauding, joking, off-hand way that was graphically described in Willis's book *Learning to Labour* (1977). The women on a parallel YTS scheme for caring for the elderly were equally dismissive of the value of their day in college, doing almost no work, refusing to co-operate and devoting their attention primarily to the rather quarrelsome relationships within the group. Drawn from unskilled working class backgrounds, their placements habituated them to tough and unattractive personal service work in retirement homes. Two BTec groups – girls learning fashion design and a mixed group on a hotel and catering course – were less overtly antagonistic to college teachers, but found the academic assignments onerous and often irrelevant. College was tolerated grudgingly, spurred partly by exaggerated expectations of the careers that might become available if successful on the course. Students, while unimpressed by tutors, were deferential, the kind of response that might be seen as appropriate, in particular, to those whose future employment was dealing with customers in hotels. The BTec students tended to come from skilled working class and lower white-collar backgrounds. Only among the A-level group did Banks *et al.* find children from professional and managerial households and only there did they find informal and personal relationships of mutual respect between teachers and students.

The correspondence between classroom relations and the social class origins of students on different post-compulsory courses, as detected by the ethnography, suggests that class background remains a very powerful determinant of careers. The paths followed after the end of compulsory schooling are thus shown to be class-confirming. However, the strength of the statistical associations between career and social class of origin are weak compared to the findings from the ethnographic component of the study. The survey evidence did indicate that entry to different career routes is class related. Educational attainment at age 16 is the principal determinant of career, but that is itself affected by social class and by the level of education of each parent. In addition, girls are higher achievers than boys. But all these factors taken together explain only a small amount (14%) of the variance in examination success.

(iii) *Identity formation*

Much of the study is about the relationship between emerging economic careers and other aspects of growing up. The transition to full adult status is slow and uneven, affected by the career route adopted.

There are some general, gender-related patterns. Girls mature sooner and pass through key life-course transitions earlier than boys, leaving single-sex groups for mixed-groups and dating rather sooner. They also have somewhat more restricted social lives, spending more time at home, and do more housework. Banks *et al.* claim that the differences were fewer than many other studies have suggested.

The authors also note differences in the domestic and social lives of young people on different career routes. Leaving home is typical for those who enter higher education, while a much more broken and uneven transition characterises others. It was not unusual for the respondents to go to live with friends for a while and then return to the parental home, but many more remained there throughout. The groups also have different leisure activities, though pubs and clubs are central to all.

One primary concern of the study was to chart the development of 'identities' among young people. (The team of researchers included both sociologists and social psychologists.) It sought to establish levels of self-esteem, which was measured in terms of a sense of *personal efficacy* ('belief in the ability to handle problems, achieve goals and deal with people effectively') and degrees of *estrangement* ('a sense of worthlessness, and meaninglessness akin to alienation'). Efficacy and estrangement were estimated by seeking self-evaluations through asking whether respondents agreed to sets of statements like: 'If I can't do a job the first time, I keep trying until I can' (agreement measures high efficacy) and 'If I could, I would be a very different person from the one I am now' (agreement would imply estrangement). Generally they found self-esteem high, except among the unemployed. Although more likely to affect girls, estrangement was generally low and was associated with low educational achievement, with being unemployed or forced into a YTS scheme, with unemployment and marital breakdown of parents, and with social isolation. Interestingly, though levels of estrangement decline slightly between 16 and 20, identity did not change much. Banks *et al.* suggest that identity is largely already formed.

(iv) *Beliefs, attitudes and political values*

Another concern of the researchers was to explore the development of a sense of citizenship and degrees of concern and involvement in public affairs. They found a considerable degree of 'teencentrism': that is, the

concerns and commitments of youth were significantly different
from those of adults. The issues that most concerned young people
were race, the roles of men and women, sex, environment, youth
training and education. On some of these there was a good deal of
agreement; the sample was generally liberal as regards sexual and
racial equality, civil rights and some aspects of welfare provision
but was conservative with regard to sex, the family and law and
order. There was thus no evidence that this generation, whose political experience was restricted to Thatcherism, had absorbed all its
values.

Some issues caused disagreement among the young people in the
sample and these included:

> . . . excessive police brutality, the pettiness of school rules, divisions
> of parental responsibilities, whether childrearing is a full-time job,
> whether politicians are motivated primarily by self-interest, whether
> teachers should have the right to strike, whether sex is alright after
> a few weeks' acquaintance, whether the church should give a clearer
> lead on sexual matters, whether homosexual relations are wrong,
> whether parents can tell you what to do while you are still living at
> home, whether adults understand young people, whether immigration
> should be halted, and, above all, whether life is so short that having
> a good time is more important than anything else.
>
> (Banks *et al.* 1992, p.132)

Banks *et al.* comment on this list, noting that 'the areas of con-
troversy are more to do with personal values and behaviour than
with relations between groups that form the substance of most political argument' (ibid., p.132). There is a clear discontinuity with the
political concerns of the adult world.

There is some relation between career routes and beliefs and
attitudes. Those who leave school earliest are most opposed to
authority and are the most politically cynical. Those who remain
in full-time education are most likely to be in favour of racial and
gender equality and to have Green attitudes. However, the differences are usually quite small. With the exception of environ-
mentalist concern, they are already in place before reaching the age
of 16.

Parents' class and education had some impact on attitudes to
more orthodox political issues. But young people, although they
intended to vote, were little interested in, and generally cynical
about, party politics. Voting intentions were volatile: '. . . fifty-seven
per cent of the sample changed their party allegiances during the
two years of the research' (ibid., p.162). There were class differences,
with middle class youth (and particularly those who were education-
ally successful) more likely to support the Conservative Party. There
were, in addition, strong regional variations, with Swindon Conservative and Liverpool Labour.

Critical Observations

One anomaly of the research was that the ethnographic study showed very considerable class differences between groups embarked on different career routes, while the survey data showed much weaker statistical associations between class and values. This might suggest that some of the methods of measuring identity are unreliable. Alternatively, it may be that the different methods produce contradictory results.

Temple (1993), while commending the use of several different methods in order to understand careers and identities, is dubious about the assumption that the several methods are consistent with one another. Perhaps different methods capture different aspects of reality? In particular, in the study of identity, Banks *et al.* tend to look for a fixed and consistent sense of self. Yet it is a truism of ethnographic research, and of interactionist theory, that meanings depend on context. Goffmann's famous book, *The Presentation of Self in Everyday Life* (1959), compels us to appreciate that people construct and transmit impressions of themselves in different contexts for different audiences. Moreover, recent writing about contemporary cultural change suggests that identities have become more fluid and that, influenced by consumer culture, people are increasingly inclined, consciously and repeatedly, to try on, and then adopt or cast aside, new identities. Such accounts contest the notion that identity is developed in a consistent way over a life time. Hence to seek a 'true', unitary, 'adult' identity, as was supposedly examined through attitude questions in the survey, is in danger of misunderstanding the very phenomena under investigation.

Allen (1993) also expresses reservations about the measuring of identity. She points out that without actually following the sample through for a longer time, it is hazardous to assume that an adult identity had been fixed into the future. It was, indeed, surprising how little identities changed between ages 16 and 20. The authors frequently claim that the on most important dimensions of attitudes, values and aspirations, young people's minds had been made up before they reached the age of 16.

Conclusion

Careers and Identities reports on a large, elaborate and important research project. It reaffirms the momentousness of the decision made at the end of compulsory schooling. But it also demonstrates that the decision is determined earlier, as pupils develop varied attitudes towards employment and authority. Those attitudes are related to their educational attainment. Choosing to stay on in full-time education is related also to family social class and to the character of post-16 provision – staying on at school was much more popular in Kirkcaldy, probably because Scottish Highers are flexible qualifications taking only one year to complete. Compared with much other recent research, the book shows rather fewer gender differences in routes, attitudes and activities within the academic system. However, once outside academic institutions, the differences became immediately and strikingly apparent just as soon as girls, at whatever age, enter a labour market strongly segregated on gender lines. Banks *et al.* give a largely persuasive account of the social dimensions of the transition from school, of the available opportunities, and of the distinctive experiences of young people in the late 1980s.

Bibliography and Further Reading

Allatt, P. and Yeandle, S. (1992), *Youth Unemployment and the Family: voices of disordered times*, London, Routledge.

Allen, S. (1992), Review of 'Careers and Identities' in *Work Employment and Society*, Vol.6, No.3, p.499.

Coffield, F., Borrill, C. and Marshall, S. (1986). *Growing Up at the Margins; young adults in the North East*, Milton Keynes, Open University Press.

Goffmann, E. (1959), *The Presentation of Self in Everyday Life*, London, Mayflower.

Temple, B. (1993), Review of 'Careers and Identities' in *Sociology*, Vol.27, No.1, pp.185–8.

Willis, P. (1977), *Learning to Labour*, Farnborough, Saxon House.

Appendices

Figure 9.1 Early career routes after completion of compulsory schooling, 1985 and 1987.

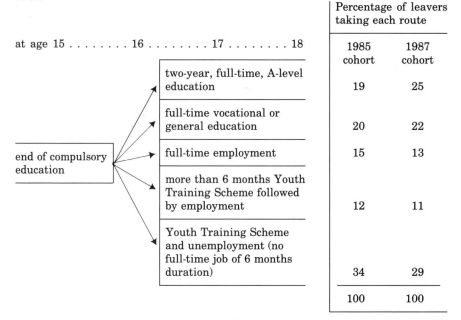

	Percentage of leavers taking each route	
at age 15 . . . . 16 . . . . 17 18	1985 cohort	1987 cohort
two-year, full-time, A-level education	19	25
full-time vocational or general education	20	22
full-time employment	15	13
more than 6 months Youth Training Scheme followed by employment	12	11
Youth Training Scheme and unemployment (no full-time job of 6 months duration)	34	29
	100	100

Source: compiled from Banks, et al (1992)

Table 9.1 Career Routes at age 16–18, by area, gender, cohort, educational qualifications at 16, and social class

| | Career Route | | | | | |
	Academic Education %	Vocational Education %	School to job %	YTS to job %	YTS/ unemployed %	n
Area:						
Swindon	21	21	29	11	18	901
Sheffield	20	17	9	16	38	947
Liverpool	20	22	11	10	37	833
Kirkcaldy	24	21	8	11	36	1014
Gender:						
Male	20	20	17	13	31	1740
Female	23	21	11	11	34	1955
Cohort:						
Older	19	20	15	12	34	2177
Younger	25	22	13	11	29	1518
Educational attainment:						
Top quartile	56	25	8	3	8	1052
2nd quartile	17	30	16	15	23	901
3rd quartile	4	18	18	19	41	846
Bottom quartile	2	8	16	12	62	882
Social class:						
Professional	50	18	9	9	14	188
Intermediate	37	26	11	9	17	618
Skilled non-manual	30	22	13	10	25	358
Skilled manual	16	21	17	13	32	1123
Partly skilled	12	17	18	14	39	521
Unskilled	16	11	14	15	43	196

(ibid., Table 3.1, p. 38)

Table 9.2 Post-18 careers by career trajectories 16–18 (%)

| | 16–18 trajectories (Type A) | | | | | |
18–20 trajectories	Academic	Vocational	Job	YTS-job	YTS/ unemployed	Total
Higher education	56	11	0	0	2	18
Other education	8	5	0	0	3	7
Employment	32	69	88	88	59	60
Unemployment	4	15	12	10	36	15

(ibid., Table 3.2, p. 40)

10

Middle Class Youth: Conformity and Rebellion

Peter Aggleton (1987), *Rebels Without A Cause*, London, The Falmer Press.

Sue Penna

The Sociology of Youth

The sociology of youth has been a growing area of sociological interest in the post-war period, with research investigating many aspects of the lives of young working class males and, more recently, young women and youth from ethnic minorities. The study of middle class youth, however, remains relatively underdeveloped and it is this gap in our understanding of young people's lives which is addressed by Aggleton's research.

Rebels Without A Cause examines the reasons for the educational underachievement of young people from 'new middle class' families. It considers the dominant form of socialization within the family; young people's experiences of, and responses to, the educational process; the forms of work these young people take and the sub-cultural contexts in which young people use their leisure time. These areas are investigated principally in order to answer two questions. The first is the theoretical question of whether youthful rebellious practices constitute symbolic forms of resistance to structural power relations. The second is the empirical question of why young middle class people should underachieve at school. It is usually assumed that young people from families rich in cultural capital succeed within the educational system. Cultural capital refers to advantages people have because of their social and educational background.

These interrelated issues cross the sociological boundaries between the sociology of education and the sociology of youth culture and sub-culture, in the critical ethnographic tradition utilised by Paul Willis in *Learning To Labour*. Young people's experience of education is considered in relation to other key aspects of their lives so that the social factors which cut across these different areas can be analysed.

Research Design

Aggleton conducted a three year ethnographic study in which data were collected through a combination of participant observation and semi-structured interviews. The sample consisted of 27 students undertaking GCE A level courses at a college of further education in southern England. A core of six students was identified by their teachers as irregular attenders who did not put much effort into their work, and the other 21 were drawn from the friendship network of this core. These students came from a total of 20 households defined as new middle class, a category characterised by 'new left' political interests such as the environment, feminism, animal rights and so on, as well as liberal views on social issues such as sex and drugs. Eleven of the households were headed by a single parent – ten of them women and one male. The majority of the parents were professional people working as teachers in primary, secondary, further or higher education, or in the media or arts. The background of the students was relatively homogeneous, with parents sharing similar lifestyles as well as occupational characteristics.

Principal Findings

The study concentrated on identifying the social practices, meanings and interactions operating across the domestic, educational and subcultural contexts of students' lives. Aggleton found that the socialization of children in the twenty new middle class households took a specific form, characterised by two main features:

(1) Strong distinctions between culturally acceptable and culturally non-acceptable practices

(2) A strong emphasis on personal autonomy and the negotiation of family relationships

These two characteristics were found to influence the ways in which students experienced their educational and subcultural contexts.

(i) *The domestic context*

The households in the sample lived in spacious houses, with typical styles of furniture, decor and food proclaiming the interests of household members. Aggleton details that the walls of rooms were often decorated with postcards, children's drawings, posters advertising arts or dance events as well as women's issues, ecological concerns and so on. A variety of objects were lying around in a jumbled fashion. These objects shared a number of characteristics; they represented individually crafted, rather than mass produced, items and reflected a preference for the foreign and exotic. Many kitchens contained pasta, rice, pulses and so on stored in jars, earthenware pottery pans and dishes and the occasional wood-burning stove.

This collection of objects and their distribution around the home denoted a set of cultural concerns which were further affirmed by parents' encouragement of particular experiences for their children. Important amongst these was foreign travel. Time was made to ensure young people had such travel experience which was always indepen- dently organized, rather than through a travel agency. Travelling abroad was not undertaken for relaxation, but to expose young people to broader cultural experiences.

Young people's cultural experiences were extended at home by the practice of taking in lodgers, guests and a permanent stream of visi- tors. This relative openness of the home to others was nevertheless highly selective with guests, visitors and lodgers being students, teachers, or involved in the arts. Conversation in the home revolved around politics, sex, drugs, and local community and arts events, rein- forcing the acceptability of particular cultural norms.

In contrast to the strong distinction between acceptable (the artistic, 'exotic' and relatively unconventional) and unacceptable (the conven- tional, 'ordinary' and mass produced) cultural practices, domestic rela- tionships were relatively open. Unlike either traditional working class or traditional middle class households, there was no clear separation between the privacy of the home and the outside world, with various guests and visitors welcomed easily.

Similarly, there were blurred boundaries between acceptable adult and child behaviours. This was evident in parents' attitudes to, and con- trol over, young people's experiences with drugs, alcohol and sexuality. As well as openly discussing the use of alcohol and drugs and sexual relationships, parents allowed young people a considerable amount of freedom. Alcohol and 'soft' drugs (marijuana) could be consumed in the home (although cigarettes were frowned upon or banned), and young people could have a sexual partner stay overnight. Parents considered that if these activities took place within the home they would be able to monitor them and stop any harmful situations from arising.

This exercise of parental control and surveillance was achieved through negotiation within the family. Aggleton documents that from an early age young people had been encouraged to stay out late at night and make their own decisions about where they went and when they ate, for example. This independence could not be taken for granted however, but had to be negotiated with parents. Parents and children gave reasons for their decisions, debating the merits, or otherwise, of particular courses of action. Such a level of personal autonomy and negotiation of personal conduct was a significant feature of the sociali- zation of children from the new middle class families in Aggleton's study.

This process operated differentially according to the gender of the young person. Girls were subject to far more intense surveillance concerning their movements and their relationships. There was a pre- occupation with ensuring daughters followed certain norms in sexual relationships, with an emphasis on monogamous and committed heterosexuality with a partner who had previously been judged suit- able by parents. Young men experienced far less of this concern with

their relationships and movements, being subjected rather to a
process of monitoring to ensure their participation in heterosexual
relationships.

(ii) *The educational context*

Parental choices in educational provision reflected their desire for a
specific form of socialization. Prior to their secondary education, 14 of
the young people had attended free schools (i.e. small, alternative
voluntary and collectively-run schools), or schools characterized by
child-centred learning processes. The emphasis of these schools was on
the development of personal autonomy and time management, with
children learning at their own pace. It was at the stage of secondary
education that many young people experienced difficulties. At 16
years, 23 of the sample wanted to leave school and attend college. This
desire was strongly related to their dislike of certain characteristics of
the school process. These were the structured use of time (timetabled
lessons, etc.,), the regimentation of space (lining up for assembly, etc.,),
and the numerous rules such as the wearing of uniform.

These characteristics were the ones that were most different from
students' experiences at home. The negotiated, person-centred, unres-
trictive characteristics of the home contrasted sharply with the
authoritarian, regimented and impersonal structures of the school.
The lack of personal autonomy within school was experienced as
irksome and illegitimate and students adopted strategies to deal with
this mismatch between home and school contexts.

These strategies were the same as those used to negotiate social situations and interactions within the home. They took the form of verbal
challenges to teachers' authority, using elaborated argument. In this
way students attempted to exert influence over the dominant values
of the school. The culturally accepted norms of the home, when transposed to the educational context, led to several conflicts. One respondent recalled that:

> ". . . You know, I used to argue with the headmistress over points. OK
> . . . the majority of points were totally trivial. But you know, just points
> of school uniform. And I did that once and had a very large argument
> with her, and got pulled up before the deputy head and got told that I
> wasn't allowed to talk to the headmistress like that . . ."
>
> (Aggleton, 1987, p.67)

Aggleton showed that the social competencies learned at home were
used to challenge, negotiate and redefine the rules and regulations of
the school, with the result that pupils were considered trouble-makers.
Aggleton argues that these disputes represent a process of contestation
between the values being used in the home and those characterizing
the school context.

The decision to transfer to college was an attempt to find an educational context which would allow students more autonomy and control. Once at college this intention to exert personal autonomy was evident in the irregular attendance of students, who managed on the whole to negotiate around such matters with their tutors. The choice of subjects at college reflected the interests valued at home – English literature, theatre studies and arts subjects were particularly popular. Other subjects – engineering, bricklaying and secretarial studies, for example – were negatively valued because they did not conform to ideas of cultural worth found within the home. They were also associated with unacceptable personal styles, aspirations and masculinities and femininities. One young man commented:

> ". . . They're all so macho those engineering 'lads' (sneer). All they ever do is go around getting pissed and trying to pick up secretaries (female students following courses of secretarial training at College). They're sort of really thick and brutish and boring . . ." (ibid., p.71)

Similarly, a young woman speaking of two fellow students said:

> ". . . Oh Sheila and Vi, they're so disgustingly twee. They're always creeping around the library, working hard on their essays and things like that, wearing those disgusting pretty skirts with flowers on them, drinking dry martinis and orange juices in the pub. They're just vile . . ." (ibid., p.74)

We can see in these quotes that the form of gender identity and style adopted by other students is negatively evaluated by the students in Aggleton's sample. At the same time, industrious application to academic work was not associated with success, which instead was seen to reside within the individual and would somehow manifest itself at the necessary time. Thus, the educational context is found by Aggleton to contain those features identified in the domestic context; a distinction between culturally acceptable and unacceptable norms and an emphasis on personal autonomy.

(iii) *The sub-cultural context*

'Sub-culture' in Aggleton's study refers to the contexts in which students were relatively free of adult supervision. Their leisure time was spent in selected pubs, clubs and arts venues. These places allowed students some control over the social interactions within them. Commercial discos and clubs were rejected because of the lack of opportunity to challenge traditional behaviours, styles and values. For example, both male and female respondents commented on the conformist, gendered behaviour found in such venues. Young men expressed concern about the possibility of violence and young women about restrictions to their autonomy (ibid., p.91).

   The criteria of control over social situations also guided employment choices. Students looked for work in particular pubs, restaurants and other places which allowed them certain freedoms; negotiating hours of employment and opportunities to meet friends, for example. As in the domestic context, and in choice of education, the students' desire to blur boundaries could be seen in attempts to transform their work contexts into personalised leisure settings.

   However, there were limits to the young people's attempts to exert personal control over instructional and social settings. Whilst young women showed an awareness of feminist politics, their personal relationships were constrained by traditional gender roles. In mixed groups Aggleton noted that young women tended to be both restrained and quiescent in their behaviour (ibid., p.104). Activities tended to be dominated, both verbally and physically, by male members of the group. When challenged by young women the males would respond by trying to insult or stigmatise them. In this sense the public challenges to dominant norms and values did not succeed at the private level, where young men exerted traditional patriarchal strategies of control over the social and instructional setting.

   A sexual double standard also operated. Young women were expected to conform to traditional, committed, monogamous heterosexual relations, whereas young men distinguished between relatively serious and casual relationships, both of which were acceptable. A small number of the sample reported a same-sex sexual experience.

Critical Observations

Whilst commentators have remarked favourably on this study (Banks, 1988, Mac an Ghaill, 1988), some reservations have been expressed. Smart (1988) raises some methodological difficulties about the ethnographic status of the study. Smart points out that the objective of ethnographic research is to present the world as it appears to, and is experienced by, the subjects of research. This was not one of Aggleton's aims; for instance, he said that his participation in the field was to 'detect the more obvious evasions and deceptions that students might employ' (ibid., p.35). The ethnographic method does not require the researcher to judge whether or not their subjects are presenting a truthful account, but to detail the meanings contained in accounts from the point of view of the subjects.

   The second point raised by Smart is the lack of gender analysis in the chapter on the home. There is a complete absence of any detail of gender relations between spouses or parents and children, making it difficult to know if both parents agreed over culturally acceptable or unacceptable practices, or who had more say in defining these things, for example. Neither do we know how the domestic division of labour was structured within these households. Whilst Aggleton detailed the way in which conventional attitudes towards sexuality were held by parents, he missed out the routines of domestic labour so that we cannot tell if other conventional gender behaviours were reproduced in daily patterns of living. Because of such omissions, the gendered form of domestic power relations remains invisible.

Conclusion

Despite these criticisms, Aggleton's study makes a substantial contribution to an under-researched area of social life (Banks, 1988; Mac an Ghaill, 1988). The empirical data is used to refine a typology of 'resistance'. The distinction Aggleton makes between *resistance* (challenges aimed at structural power relations) and *contestation* (challenges aimed at control features of specific, local settings) provides a more solid sociological base for the study of youthful rebellion than the single overarching concept of 'resistance'. By demonstrating that the rebellious behaviour of his sample was confined to specific situations in which their ability to exert personal control was circumscribed, Aggleton is able to show the theoretical limitations of conceiving of rebellious youth as agents of social transformation. Indeed, the way in which these young people interpreted the behaviour of others within a cultural frame of reference specific to the new middle class suggests that their interpretations of, and attitudes towards, working class practices serve to reinforce class, as well as gender, divisions. We can also see from this study that there are differences in values and norms *within* as well as *between* classes. The categories of 'working class' or 'middle class' are therefore unlikely to refer to a homogenous social group. In Aggleton's study, young people from the new middle class rebelled against many traditional middle class norms, whilst also conforming to others.

Bibliography

Banks, O. (1988), Review Symposium, in *British Journal of Sociology of Education*, Vol.9, No.2, pp.223–226.
Mac an Ghaill, M. (1988), Review Symposium, *ibid.*, pp.226–230.
Smart, C. (1988), Review Symposium, *ibid*, pp.231–233.
Willis, P. (1977), *Learning To Labour*, Farnborough, Saxon House.

11

Unemployment, Young People and Family Life

Patricia Allatt and Susan Yeandle (1992), *Youth Unemployment and the Family: Voices of Disordered Times*, London, Routledge.

Roger Walters

The Sociology of Youth Unemployment

The 1980s was characterised by recession and almost constantly rising unemployment. North East England is again one of the areas hardest hit by recession and the decline of 'traditional' manufacturing industry – shipbuilding, coal, steel and railways pre-eminent amongst them. We are also in a period of growing unrest within the family. There has, for many years, been talk of the 'decline' of the family, of stress in family life, of an increase in divorce and separation and of a growing number of one-parent families. Furthermore, young people in general, and youth subcultures in particular, have been defined by successive generations, as a 'problem'. Allatt and Yeandle uniquely bring together these 'problem' areas of unemployment, the family and youth, through empirical research set in an area of Newcastle upon Tyne during the 1980s.

Their research focusses on the conjunction of two types of social change within the setting of family life. The first concerns changes associated with the life-course – transitions to schooling, work, marriage and parenthood which occur primarily within or through the family situation. The second type relates to societal change; in particular a restructured labour market and high rates of youth unemployment brought about by economic and technological change. The family, youth and unemployment are examined through the management of change during the transitional years between the 'end of childhood' and the 'entry into adulthood'. In the process, family members exchange relationships through speech, through the deployment of resources, and through transactions and negotiations which 'texture' people's lives. The nub of the study concerns how family members deal with personal change and with the generational divide in the midst of a harsh economic climate, how this conjunction of change is mediated within the structure of family relationships, and how this impinges upon the wider society.

Consequently, this research relates specifically to two key, problematic concepts – social change and continuity. The juxtaposing of these processes is exemplified here by unemployment on the one hand, the family on the other. In particular, industrial, technological, economic and social changes make unemployment an important political issue. Social problems such as crime, ill-health, divorce and poverty have been exacerbated by its rise. Unemployment has also fomented social and industrial conflicts, including inner city riots and the Miners Strike in 1984. It threatens individuals, families, communities, institutions and, despite recent election results, even the fabric of government itself. Allatt and Yeandle focus on the deleterious effects of unemployment; the instability, anxiety and uncertainty; the challenge to deeply held values associated with the work ethic; questions of fairness and equality and the threat to moral order. They argue that generally this results in a 'disordered' society in which individuals find it extremely difficult to make sense of their lives.

Research Design

The study, conducted between 1983 and 1985, examined responses to economic change amongst a sample of 40 families living in Eldon, the fictional name given to an area in Newcastle upon Tyne. The young people involved in the study had either recently left school or entered the labour market at 16 years old. About 11,000 people were living there. Housing, 90% of which was owned by the local authority, generally dated from the 1930s. It included pockets of 'junk housing', used to absorb problems of homelessness, and generally was characterised by poor housing, overcrowding, and old and inadequate amenities. A decline in local employment opportunities was paralleled by a growth in crime, mostly car theft, petty burglary and housebreaking. Between 1978 and 1981 the male unemployment rate for men aged 16–64 had risen from 16.0% to 29.6%, whilst 12.5% of economically active women aged 16–59 were also unemployed.

The advantages of locating the research in Eldon ward were twofold. First, it was a more self-contained and stable ward, in terms of population movements, than others in Newcastle. Second, evidence from a variety of sources – including local government officials, teachers, youth workers and the police – suggested that this was a neighbourhood which had been held in high regard by local people for many years.

The sample of 40 was selected from 240 families living in Eldon. Selection criteria included household composition, current employment status, whether young people were still at home, employment history and disability. Families of the disabled were excluded since the pilot study had shown this to be an additional burden. Families were matched on the age, sex and education of the key informant. The additional variables of employment status of family members, and size of family, raised problems and resulted in two groups. First, a core group of two-parent families in which all members over 16 were in full-time employment or full-time education (with the exception of the mother). Second, a group of families in which members had experienced unemployment either in the present or the past. Sampling difficulties derived from shifts and changes in the economy and labour market which had seriously affected people's lives.

Information was obtained from the sample of families by means of interview. The mother was interviewed first. It was assumed that she was the family member most likely 'to be aware of the internal dynamics of family relationships' (Allatt and Yeandle, 1992, p.161). The interview schedules covered the following areas: labour market and work; networks; domestic division of labour; peer group; authority and control within the family; household day; family resources; education; health; family history; and voting. Allatt and Yeandle did not want to impose themes. These were present in, and emerged from, people's responses. This is a key point in ethnographic research. Furthermore Allatt and Yeandle maintain that an item that occurs once is as important to the analysis as one that occurs many times. The study was not, as a result, statistically representative.

Principal Findings

The researchers looked at the effects of social change on one particular area in the North East. Their findings are, in one sense, parochial. In another sense, as Allatt and Yeandle maintain, 'it speaks for a much wider population' (ibid., p. 142). In other words, we can generalize from the findings, especially since 'the impact of technological and economic change, particularly in the effect upon labour markets, has been felt throughout British society' (ibid., p.142).

There are six main findings, as follows:

(i) Their evidence tends to suggest that restructured labour markets impinge on other people's lives besides those who are immediately affected. For example, Allatt and Yeandle found that 'the anxieties, fears and behaviours which flow from a poor labour market and which are particularly evident in families where young members are without jobs are also found in families apparently untouched by unemployment' (ibid., p.142). Mrs Freeman exemplifies the latter. Her family and close relatives are virtually all in full-or part-time employment. Yet she said:

'I tend to worry, I worry about their future and things like that ... When Mark [her son] was coming up to leaving school and you knew that things were bad, I used to say, 'if only he gets a job I'll be the happiest woman on earth'. Fortunately he did, but then there's no guarantee that he's going to keep the job.'   (ibid., p.29, brackets added)

(ii) The intersection of a restructured local labour market and changes in the transitional stage between adolescence and adulthood are mediated within the family. The research findings indicate a number of effects of this. These include the uncertainties resulting from a poor labour market, the postponement of young people's independence in the family context and the changes in employment status of young members which reflected their powerlessness. This was further exacerbated by the extension of parental power into the world of work, whereby families used their knowledge and other resources to help their young members into the labour market. Parents who found work for their children meant an obligation on the latter, and a responsibility for good performance on the former. As Mr Page, having found work for his son, explained:

'Well the first thing they ask is, "Is he any good? Is he a decent timekeeper?" Well if they are, if you show them that well, you stand a guarantee for them sort of style. If you weren't too sure of a person ... well you wouldn't ask for him in. Every bad move they make looks on to you.'   (ibid., p.133)

What these effects represented was a reconstruction of the social order by which we give shape and meaning to our lives, a renegotiation of the boundaries of control, and a disruption to life-course expectations through the denial of economic and social resources provided for young people by paid employment. Such change not only means stress, tension and bewilderment, but it highlights contradictions and the prioritizing of values. Ultimately, what Allatt and Yeandle found was a complex range of responses by families, which amounted to varying degrees of coping, adaptation and resignation (see *Passage 11.1*, p.110).

(iii) Allatt and Yeandle show that a poor labour market can affect family life in quite intimate ways. Time, for example, was experienced differently by employed and unemployed members of a family. Not only did the latter tend to get in the way of the former, but they were not as constrained by time. Furthermore, the unemployed member had little to contribute to family conversation at the end of the day. Consequently they could become the subject of teasing and banter which reflected their subservient status in the family hierarchy and they were thrust outside the patterns and routines of the everyday world which foster and signify belonging. Such displacement meant being consigned to a lower order of membership, one in which the structures of time, work and money not only produced a moral order from which they were excluded, but also one which their condition challenged. 'Unemployment posed a threat to the way some perceived the proper order to the world, creating embarrassment and a tendency to blame the individual' (ibid., p.144). In summary then, the unemployed were denied routines, work and money. They lacked an externally imposed structure to the day, they were in the way of those in employment and they became displaced from family discourse. Such findings serve to highlight the deep sense of frustration, tinged with anger and anxiety, felt by many unemployed young people in the North East.

(iv) Structural change also exposed contradictions in cultural values in families and in the community. It did so in four ways. First, it created material and emotional uncertainty. Second, it highlighted ambiguities in cultural values, for instance a tendency toward particularistic, rather than universalistic, concerns based on notions of equity and fairness and exemplified in the response that 'when jobs were scarce families had to look after their own' (ibid., p.144). Third, 'traditional' values were also exposed in terms of gender and domestic division of labour issues (see *Passage 11.1*, p.110). Who had most need of a job, when future family responsibilities were accounted for, challenged the ideal of equality. This was particularly evident in the conversation between Stephen Woods, who was unemployed, and his 19 year old girlfriend, the mother of his child. He was anxious for them to set up home together.

> *Girlfriend*: 'I says to him, "Why should I work?" when he should work. He should support wer, not me support him and the bairn, then meself. Like if he got a job, I would like get a part-time job when she's one or two.'
> *Stephen*: 'But you've got a better chance of getting a proper job 'cos you're the lass. Lasses can be on supermarket tills and what have you. You could get a start tomorrow, but they wouldn't start me there with us having a criminal record and that.'   (ibid., p.127)

Fourth, the work ethic was challenged. The fact that it was possible, albeit inadequately, to carve out an existence on social security, contradicted some people's sense of what was proper and legal. Furthermore, when some young people were just about able to do this whilst still living at home, some parents worried that their children might grow accustomed to an existence on social security. They would thus lose the urge to work. Mrs Robson said:

> 'It's easy for people to get into a rut if you *start* off your life not knowing what work is but you're still going to get kept. Maybe it's a minimum, but you're still getting kept aren't you? It might be easy to go that way.'
>   (ibid., p.80)

Against this, families attempted to provide support for their young. They drew on time, money, patience, authority, contacts and knowledge, and tried to sustain a notion of fairness between siblings. Sometimes work status would hold sway over such notions, but 'they had to prepare their children for a changing world whilst attempting to sustain those beliefs and practices they valued' (ibid., p.145).

(v) Allatt and Yeandle also found that notions of trust and reciprocity remained important in family life, but that structural change had detrimentally affected this. Young people felt let down – by society, by the state and by government. There was a deep sense that 'a modern wealthy society owes more to its younger members and that with political will this could be achieved' (ibid., p.145). They also argue that even with profound economic change in Eastern and Western Europe, the place of the young in the new economic order remains uncertain. Those without economic resources are in danger of being 'socially dislodged and disconnected from both large and small social units which constitute a society' (ibid., p.146).

(vi) Finally, there is little sense of anomie amongst youth in this research. In contrast, researchers such as Cashmore (1984) argued that the pressure and frustration of deprivation can lead to a state of anomie, for working class people in particular. In portraying youth in the early 1980s being denied access to the possession of goods previously obtained through working, earning and spending, Cashmore maintains that unemployed young people experience a disjuncture between the cultural goal of consumption and the opportunity channels through which this goal can be achieved. Anomie, internalising or accepting goals which cannot be achieved, did not seem to be a characteristic of youth in Eldon in the early 1980s.

In summary, this research focused on *change* as exemplified by unemployment, restructured local labour markets, transitions in the life-course, and a growing need for young people to be independent. This was juxtaposed with *order*, particularly in the ways in which the above aspects challenged and undermined it. Order means making sense of our lives through moral values, notions of fairness, equality and trust. Yet unemployment left young people feeling frustrated, dependent upon others, and with a sense of disorder which undermined a feeling of belonging. Job shortages and chronic anxiety about obtaining and retaining paid employment brought to the fore contradictions in values, associated with equity, equality, gender and fairness. There was a sense of being out of time, out of place, unemployment rupturing the sequencing of life-course events. This feeling is shown in Mr Phillip's account of his own, and his son's, reaction to sudden unemployment:

'You feel sick. I mean you say, "Oh hell. Well what the hell is he going to do now? He's just 20-year-old and where'll he get a job?" You just feel a bit sick. Plus, I mean, he's got his car now, he's courting strong and all of a sudden he goes from getting on, and enjoying himself, buying a car, to *nothing* and it's a big, big drop. He's been bad-tempered and moody since he got finished and that's just in a month'.

(ibid., p.95)

Such feelings are encapsulated in the subtitle of the book – *Voices of Disordered Times*. Thus 'whilst older workers referred to themselves and their lives as being finished, younger people could not rely on even starting theirs' (ibid., p.95). In this situation Allatt and Yeandle see resources playing a significant role in constituting the give and take of family life. Resources can, after all, have many uses. They can be accumulated, converted, wasted, bartered, borrowed, invested, given, lent, and used as bribery or emotional blackmail. Certain resources, are particularly important, such as: time; space; domestic labour; economic, social, cultural and emotional capital. Examining such resources within the family context can provide a means of challenging ways of conceptualising the unemployed, Allatt and Yeandle argue.

Evaluation

This is an important piece of research. It traces a number of problems associated with the transition from youth to adulthood. These are examined within the context of the family and against a background of rising unemployment in a restructured, and poor, local labour market. In particular, Allatt and Yeandle are concerned with the effects these problems have had on relationships within the family. Consequently they provide detailed discussion on the interrelationship between youth, the family and unemployment, an area which has hitherto been little researched by sociologists. They provide statistical data from official, and other, secondary sources, (see *Table 11.1*, p.109) and from the research (see *Table 11.2*, p.110). This is combined with first-hand accounts conveying the feeling of living amidst the crisis of unemployment.

Whilst Allatt and Yeandle examine, with sensitivity, relationships within the family across generations, their study seems to have 'fallen between two stools'. They try to cover too much. Consequently, in parts, they appear to scratch the surface. They have not provided a clear, in-depth, analysis of the problems exemplified by previous empirical work in these areas. In fairness, researchers such as Fagin and Little (1984) examined the family and unemployment, whilst Cashmore (1984) looked at youth and unemployment but neither analysed the conjunction of these three areas.

There is nevertheless a lack of depth in certain aspects. For example, during a period in which juvenile crime is attracting media attention in proportions amounting to 'moral panic', there are few references to the relationship between this and unemployment. Apart from one couple in the study, who tried to influence their son against mixing with people engaged in petty crime, the effects of crime on relationships within the family gets little attention. Reasons for this could include; first, that the sample was unrepresentative of juvenile criminals; second, that the researchers were concerned with 'ordinary kids' rather than those committing juvenile crime; or third, that some respondents chose not to mention their illegal activities.

Allatt and Yeandle take a sociological and historical perspective in examining change and continuity. Whilst they discuss unemployment from within an historical perspective, this is not so in the case of youth. Indeed, there seems little material on youth during the postwar decades. This was a time during which, arguably, adolescence and youth were 'constructed' in terms of a high, free spending generation. In the North East, as elsewhere, youth was associated with teddy boys, hippies, skinheads, racism, football hooliganism, etc. Elements of this are not reflected in this book. This could be because the book is about 'ordinary kids', who are probably the majority. If so, it would also serve to explain the low priority given to crime. Nevertheless, this does raise the issues of whether subcultures have disappeared, changed substantially, or whether new forms of resistance have arisen? Also we need to ask how much young respondents have been prepared to divulge to the researchers, a point raised earlier. Looked at objectively, Allatt and Yeandle's work reflects a 'snapshot in time', the mid-1980s. Perhaps we should not expect too much in the way of an historical context even though ethnography has been criticised for this omission.

Ethnographic approaches such as this are not able to examine relative frequencies, test causal relationships between variables, or make generalizations from the findings. The sample of 40 families was relatively small. Not all research, and especially ethnographic research, is necessarily geared towards generalization. Nevertheless, we do need to examine closely the basis on which the families were selected. We need to ask whether there was sufficient reason given for excluding those in which there were disabled people, a group already on the margins of society. The decision to exclude such families seems strange in the light of a concern with family relationships; an opportunity has been missed through a concern on the researchers' part to keep the number of variables as low as possible.

Conclusion

In focusing on unemployment Allatt and Yeandle have opened up a number of related themes including poverty, class, gender, age, the family, the State, crime, health, education, vocational training and the mass media. They examine relationships in families across generations. They analyse the often complex responses to unemployment of young, and not so young, women and men. Although a sense of anger and outrage seems to be lacking from young people in these 40 families, this does not necessarily reflect a mood of resignation and acceptance amongst them. They are not losing the capacity to fight back, but, despite the enormity of the problems, they are utilising their resources to cope and adapt.

Bibliography and Further Reading

Allatt, P. and Yeandle, S. (1986), *It's Not Fair Is It?: Youth Unemployment, Family Relations and the Social Contract*, in Allen *et al.* (eds.) (below).

Allen, S. *et al.* (eds.) (1986), *The Experience of Unemployment*, London, Macmillan.

Cashmore, E.E. (1984), *No Future: Youth and Society*, London, Heinemann.

Cusack, S. and Roll, J. (1985), *Families Rent Apart: A Study of Young People's Contributions to their Parents' Housing Costs*, London, Child Poverty Action Group and Youthaid.

Fagin, L. and Little, M. (1984), *The Forsaken Families*, Middlesex, Penguin.

Lewis, P. (1985), *Introduction: Policies Towards Young People* in Cusack and Roll (above)

Mungham, G. (1982), *Workless Youth as Moral Panics* in Rees, and Atkinson, (eds.) (below)

Rees, T. L. and Atkinson, P. (eds.) (1982), *Youth Unemployment and State Intervention*, London, RKP.

Willis, P. (1973), *Learning to Labour: How Working Class Kids Get Working Class Jobs*, London, Saxon House.

Willis, P. (1984), 'Youth Unemployment: A New Social State', in *New Society*, 29 March.

Willis, P. (1984), 'Youth Unemployment: Ways of Living', in *New Society*, 5 April.

Willis, P. (1984), 'Youth Unemployment: The Land of Juventus', in *New Society*, 12 April.

Appendices

Table 11.1 Unemployment in Great Britain by age, July 1979 and July 1984

Age	1979	Number Unemployed 1984	% Change
Under 18	258,700[c]	158,966[a]	
18–19	131,200	336,173	+156
20–24	225,500	658,901	+192
25 and over	776,700	1,824,853[b]	+135
Total	1,392,100	2,978,893	+135

Source: Department of Employment *Employment Gazette* (May 1980 and September 1984, cited in Lewis 1985:3).

Notes:
a Excludes 163,000 school-leavers and 283,151 on the Youth Training Scheme.
b Excludes some men over 60.
c Excludes 68,500 on the Youth Opportunities Programme.
(Allatt and Yeandle, 1992, Table 1.2, p. 16)

Table 11.2 Number of jobs held by young people in the sample since leaving school

Number of jobs	Females	Males	Total
0	5	8	13
1	9	8	17
2	1	3*	4
3 or more	2*	4*	6
Total	17	23	40

Note: *The figures include some part-time jobs.
(ibid., Table 2.5, p.53)

Passage 11.1

The comments of Caroline Price, a young clerical worker, reveal the complexities of the issue of fairness in the division of labour between the sexes. Here the ambiguities of equality and gender roles are shaped by personal experience and family circumstances. The extract follows Caroline's statement that she did not want to marry anyone who was unemployed.

'Me brother did that before. They're separated now but she worked all the time and he stayed in the house and did all the cooking and clearing up. I think it's one of the reasons why they separated because I think she started to resent him because he wasn't working. "You should be the one that's working", type of thing. "I should be able to maybe stay off work and do the housework and have a baby." She did actually start saying to him, "I'm not giving you no more money, you're not going out tonight." And she was the only place where he could get money from. You know, if your husband says to you, "Please give me a fiver so I can go out", it's not very nice. I think if I did eventually get married and that, I wouldn't want to work. I think that's another reason why there's not so many jobs as well, it's because women do men's jobs these days and I don't think that's such a good thing after all. Even they are driving the buses now, women. You don't see many of them mind. I think I have always seen me mam go out to work and she has always worked, and then she will come dashing in and get the tea ready. And me dad, although he does a lot of things round the house, he always seems to still get that bit waited on, and I think when me mam's working that's not right. But if she wasn't working you know, well that's her job and that's his job. As long as he is sort of paying her to do it, paying her all the housekeeping and that, plus like her extra to do it, I think that's great. I mean it worked for hundreds and hundreds of years, why not have a go?'

(ibid., pp.127–128)

12

Adultery

Annette Lawson (1988), *Adultery: An Analysis of Love and Betrayal*, Oxford, Blackwell.

Pauline Hare

Marriage is one of several social institutions deemed (correctly or not) to help maintain social order. From this point of view, adultery may be seen as the underside of marriage – another institution, but hidden and deviant. For many centuries adultery was considered both a sin and a crime; indeed in some parts of the Western world it remains on the statute books as a crime. It was also, for many centuries, the *only* grounds for divorce and, in addition, was also defined *only as the act of a married woman.* A husband's extra-marital liaisons were deemed neither adulterous nor criminal.

Despite, however, its long history and current prevalence; despite its durability as a theme for novels, plays, films, songs, etc.; despite the public's apparent fascination with the adulteries, real or imagined, of princes, politicians, and plebians; academically, adultery has most commonly been written about only as a side-issue of research on marriage and personal relationships. Very rarely has it been addressed as the primary topic of investigation.

Adultery: An Analysis of Love and Betrayal seeks to remedy this omission. Inquiring about relationships and marriages, both faithful and adulterous, it considers, amongst other things: the links between people's beliefs and attitudes and their behaviour; how these may alter with time and/or changes in marital status; gender differences in attitudes and behaviour; the various outcomes of adulterous behaviour; some possible reasons for changes in behaviour, including the impact on women of paid employment outside the home; and, pervading all of the above, the notion of 'power'.

Just as previous studies of marriage could not ignore the impact of adultery on emotional and physical relationships, so this work on adultery is, inevitably, also a study of marriage, as affected by the reality or the possibility of adulterous behaviour. Lawson's work links the stability of marriage to traditional fields of enquiry concerning the creation and maintenance of social stability thus: 'Adultery is all about the setting, breaking, or maintaining and the creation of boundaries. It is about breaching the social order, about transgression . . . In the breach of the rule is the rule made clear, by studying adultery . . . marriage may be better understood' (Lawson, 1988, p. 32).

Research Design

Data collection was undertaken throughout England, Scotland and Wales during 1981 and 1982 and, because Lawson wanted 'both figures and stories', she used quantitative and qualitative methods. Early unstructured interviews provided the ideas for a more formal questionnaire. Pursuing Lawson's desire for stories as well as figures, some respondents were involved further, in either in-depth interviews or small-group discussions.

Newspaper articles, written by Lawson and based in part on the early interviews, appealed for respondents. From the replies Lawson identified a target sample to whom the questionnaires were posted (for more details see Appendix B in her book) and 579 completed questionnaires were returned (a 66% response rate). Despite her efforts to include a proportionate number of men in her target sample (she surveyed all men, all couples, and only one in three women of those who had replied to her appeals), in Lawson's 'effective' sample (the 579) the ratio of women to men was still 59:41 (rather than 51:49 – the national ratio). The sample was, by occupation, overwhelmingly middle class (82% as compared to 48% of the national population), and also more highly educated than the national population (the men in the sample being better educated than the women). The sample follows the national pattern fairly closely in terms of geographical location, and regarding rural and urban areas. 100 of the 579 were involved in either interviews or discussion groups.

Her early investigations having revealed an amazingly diverse understanding of the term 'adultery', a diversity confirmed by the newspaper responses, the questionnaire specified which 'behaviours' she wished to investigate, ('. . . the long affair, the one-night stand or visit to a prostitute, or the affair of the heart only' (ibid., p.354)) and the term Lawson chose to embrace these activities was 'adulterous liaison(s)'. Of her questionnaire respondents 27% had had no such liaison; 42%, one to three; and 31%, four or more.

Particularly interesting was her decision about how to ask people questions about a taboo subject, in this case adultery. Previous work on marriage and relationships had spoken of the 'extra-marital' or 'co-marital' relationship, rather than of adultery, with its illicit connotations. Lawson, however, deliberately used the term adultery because she '. . . wanted not to avoid but to point to its long history as sin and crime and, further, to dramatize the greater sin, the greater punishment inflicted on the married woman – that is, on the adulteress as opposed to the adulterer. In this sense, "adultery" is a feminist issue . . .' (ibid., p.352).

Principal Findings

(i) *Types of adultery*

Lawson identifies three types of adulterous behaviour:
Parallel adultery, a form more commonly practised by married men than by married women, occurs when the adulterous relationship is well known and even accepted by the wife, and in which, often, the mistress is (at least partially) financially dependent on the man, and also sexually active exclusively with him. Thus the adulterous relationship mirrors rather than breaches the marriage vows.
Traditional adultery is considered a breach of the marriage vows and so, at least at first, is kept secret. This type of adultery is most commonly practised, Lawson claims, by married women: 'Where material life is dependent on marriage, discretion must cover this illicit relationship' (ibid., p.53).
Parallel and traditional adultery are seen as 'supportive' rather than as dangerous – as either 'making up the gaps' in the marital relationship and/or reassuring the individual of their worth.
Recreational adultery, in contrast, is seen as a way of living a little dangerously without risking everything of value. These liaisons are aimed at pleasure, and are usually brief and light-hearted rather than serious relationships.

(ii) *Attitudes to, and frequency of, adultery*

Whilst acknowledging and allowing for the possible impact of a decrease in women's reluctance to admit to adultery, as well as more general changes in the language used to describe intimate relationships since the late 1960s, Lawson concludes that, by comparison with Hunt's American study of 1969, '. . . men have reduced the number of their "casual affairs" while women have become readier to engage in them' (ibid., p.39). Certain social and cultural changes help to explain the new patterns:

(a) pre/post marital link

Existing studies (Atwater, 1982) show a strong link between the incidence of premarital and extramarital sexual behaviour. Lawson's results not only appear to confirm this pre/post marital link but also suggest that the greater the number and variety of premarital lovers the more numerous will be extra-marital liaisons.

(b) two 'revolutions'

Lawson identifies two social processes ('revolutions') which have contributed to this phenomenon. First, she suggests that a *sexual revolution* has taken place the result of which is that women:

- are less likely to be virgins at marriage;
- have more sexual partners than earlier generations;
- are almost as likely as men to have committed adultery;
- are catching up with men with regard to the number of adulterous liaisons;
- are increasingly likely to describe their affairs as 'casual' or 'one-night stands' (at a time when men are describing their liaisons less often in this way than previously).

In appropriating behaviours previously perceived as male, a pattern emerges which Lawson calls the *masculinization of sex.* Secondly, there has been a *talking revolution*, a broad general cultural trend, associated with the 'information society' in which we now live, which values communication and speech. Between couples this general trend is transposed into a more specific activity, 'the telling business', by which '. . . knowledge has become the new commodity of exchange between intimate partners . . . Women have always valued speech, talk, and communication as the way to intimacy . . . men are [now] talking and telling more . . . I think this trend is well termed the *feminization of love'* (ibid., p.29; my emphasis).

(c) work

Lawson hypothesizes that men and women's feelings about themselves and about each other have changed as a consequence of women's increasing participation in paid employment and that these changes would inevitably affect their sexual patterns and personal relationships.

(d) values and myths

In her investigation of love, marriage and adultery, Lawson makes reference to three great 'myths', which have arisen in different historical periods. First, 'the great European myth of adultery' (illustrated by the tale of Tristan and Isolde). Second, the 'great modern myth – the Myth of Romantic Marriage' (which is the conventional form of marriage infused by the myth of Romantic Love – i.e. total commitment to both love and sexual exclusivity). Third, and most recently, the 'Myth of Me' (which manifested itself most strongly as a consequence of the 1960s search for self-knowledge, self-actualisation and personal fulfillment).

   A conflict between the two modern myths is almost inevitable for those who try to pursue both concurrently. In an age when self-knowledge is deemed 'morally good', when '. . . passion promises the power of self-awareness in a way that is qualitatively different from other paths to such enlightenment' (ibid, p.20), and when developing the self by an exploration of every facet of the self, including one's sexuality, is unlikely to be accomplished with just one life partner, then for the individual who also entered marriage intending it to be forever, adultery appears to be one way of resolving the conflict.

Lawson suggests that 'class differentiates adulterous experience less than do gender and age' (ibid., p.356), and illustrates this by the gender differences she discovers in the working of these myths. For example, fewer women than men described their liaisons as 'one-night stands', 'brief encounters' or 'casual affairs', and those who did, claims Lawson, were most committed to the Myth of Me. By contrast, she suggests, the men who described their liaisons thus were the most traditional men, those most strongly committed to the Myth of the Romantic Marriage. This indicates, she argues, the greater seriousness of a wife's adultery: '. . . she commits adultery generally only when her feelings are deeply involved or likely to become so – the risks are too great for her to *play* as he can – while he is entitled to his "bit on the side"' (ibid., p.39).

(e) the media

The impact of the media and its role in the dissemination of both behavioural norms and of social myths is not ignored. Lawson identifies an inherent contradiction. On the one hand: 'One of the most important of the narratives told by television is . . . the story of adultery – not . . . just in fictional, dramatic form but also in talk shows and interviews' (ibid., p.20). On the other hand, the myth of Romantic Marriage is perpetuated and enhanced by constant attention being given to the lives of famous people.

(iii) Outcomes of adultery

When they marry, the vast majority of people expect to be faithful themselves and expect their spouses will in turn be faithful (see *Figure 12.1*, p.119); sexual exclusivity is right, adultery is wrong. Often, however, in practice, people tolerate sexual infidelity: over half of the marriages beset by adultery did not end in divorce. Some of the married couples (more often when the husband had strayed!) try to sort things out, not by 'going back' (an impossibility according to the study participants) but by '. . . discussing everything – in order to achieve a new and more mature intimacy' (ibid., p.296).

Some marriages are maintained by the admission of the lover into a *menage à trois*. In some cases this allows the married couple to experiment by 'expanding their own parameters' but with no intention of breaking the marriage. In other cases the arrangement permits one married partner (often the 'victim/innocent') to quietly and unofficially separate mentally, emotionally, and possibly financially, from their spouse. Despite the inherent instability and insecurity in these arrangements for at least one of the three, if roles are clearly defined they may remain stable for long periods. Sometimes, indeed, if the triangle is not maintained, both relationships collapse, for the adulterous relationship is found to depend on the obstacle (the marriage) being there.

Almost half the marriages which experienced adultery did end in divorce (compared to under 30% of the 'faithful' marriages), and the more liaisons that had occured the more likely was a divorce. Of those who did divorce only 10% married their current lovers: others remarried someone else, and some never remarried after divorce.

Again gender patterns emerged. More women than men never remarried. Men were less likely to separate after one liaison than were women. Divorced men and women currently married to an adulterous partner viewed sexual fidelity differently: the men stressed sexual fidelity less than all other categories, whereas the women seemed strongly recommitted to this ideal, sometimes more so than they had been 'the first time around'.

An emerging pattern for second marriages was also identified. Though more faithful up to the time of the study, the pattern of men having more affairs than women (as in first marriages) continues. Moreover, if they do have affairs, they have more than they did before, despite having being married for less time.

Lawson suggests that gender differences like these, in both belief and behaviour, occur because men and women's subjective experiences of similar events tends to vary. Despite the masculinization of sex which the study exposes, the increased number of women who engage in adulterous liaisons '. . . still have fewer liaisons than men and . . . experience their adultery as more serious' (ibid., p.291).

(iv) *Power, control and inequality*

Whilst, in marriage, men have traditionally held power over women, in the adulterous affair this relationship of power may be reversed. A woman may take, use, and reject her lover at her pleasure. With regard to her husband: 'In taking . . . a lover, these women cuckolded their husbands – an exercise of power of a kind even if the men remained ignorant of it' (ibid., p.53). However, Lawson's overall analysis and commentary throughout the book continually questions the extent of any new-found female power in personal relationships arising as a consequence of adulterous liaisons.

Though women may now speak more openly about their liaisons, this can be perceived as a liberation of language that, in fact, 'ends by conforming to a male model that offers only trivial freedoms to women' (ibid., p.39). Furthermore, the trends revealed as a consequence of the masculinization of sex seem to make women 'appear *like* men and, in some cases, *as if* they were men. Certainly these changes appear to conform to male rather than female models of heterosexuality and to meet the needs and desires of men better than those of women' (ibid., p.29).

Admitting to a liaison may have negative consequences for women. 'Telling' may not be altruistic, but rather a way of using emotional power against the spouse, whilst relieving guilty feelings. The study reveals that men believe their confessions will make little difference to their marriages, and this indeed turns out to be so. The exact opposite is true for women who, correctly, believe that 'telling' will jeopardise their marriage. Indeed, '. . . the cultural and structural changes in women's position as wives and mothers and at work have not permitted such [sexual] liberation as there has been to go unpunished . . . The liberated – whether female, black, or homosexual – threaten the *status quo* because they have become empowered. In practice they still have little power relative to the male, white, or heterosexual community, but even the idea that there could be movement in the power structures is threatening' (ibid., p.309).

Evaluation

Critical reactions to Lawson's book have been mixed. For Bhugra (1989) it shows 'flashes of insight', but is predictable; for Brannen (1990) it provides 'food for thought, as well as much to fascinate and with which to argue; while Drabella (1988) talked 'of its multiple strengths'. Doubts have been expressed, however, about aspects of its methodology, about some of the data analysis and about its adequacy as a feminist account.

Lawson's sample has caused concern. People who respond to appeals in newspapers, and then agree to fill in questionnaires and be interviewed, *want* to talk about the subject matter. This raises questions about representativeness and is compounded by the fact that the sample was '59% female . . . overwhelmingly middle-class, more highly educated, and more skewed to middle age than the general British population' (Atwater, 1990, p.564). The apparent increased frequency of adulterous liaisons in general, and of women's in particular, may be, in part at least, a consequence of the sampling technique. The questionnaire itself has also been criticised. It is 34 pages long, and complex: Oakley (1990, p.41) complained that 'it takes a PhD to find your way round it' and it expects an enormous range of detail from the respondents. In addition, given the sensitivity with which the topic of adultery was approached, I was personally taken aback by the stark manner in which respondents were asked to note the deaths of any of their children (contained in question 10(b)). Could this life event not have been more sympathetically addressed, perhaps by including an explanation of the need for this information?

Some reviewers pronounced many of the findings 'obvious'; for example, 'that the 1960s and 1970s were the most liberal times' or 'that more women were likely to feel guilty than men' (Bhugra, 1989, p.875). Perhaps an opportunity was missed by not attempting a separate analysis of the 45 (out of 579) working class respondents. Brannen (1990, p.323) expressed concern about 'some rather sweeping, general conclusions' which she attributed to the blending of qualitative and quantitative approaches. She also suggested that 'the multifarious strands of the argument tend at times to get lost in the discussion of the data', a view shared by Bhugra.

The main reservations, however, revolve around the issue of feminist scholarship. Brannen considered issues of gender inadequately formulated in the research design and that Lawson's largely middle class sample might underestimate the negative aspects of women's experience of adultery. She was also suspicious of Lawson's claim to have chosen to use the term 'adultery' on the grounds, claimed as specifically feminist, that it would 'dramatise "the greater sin" of "the adultress"'. Oakley too was disappointed with the book's 'theoretical and ideological orientation'. A 'systematic and thoughtful exploration of the – clearly crucial – gender issues' is prevented, she declared, by the use of phrases which suit a popular American market, like 'the masculinization of sex'. In Oakley's view, Lawson only 'hovers on the edge of any hard-hitting analysis'.

Nevertheless, Brannen acknowledged that the book addresses some important issues, such as that of the impact of disclosure, and its relationship to power, control and inequality. In addition, she welcomed the 'great number of historical and literary anecdotes' which transform an empirical study into a 'rich piece of scholarship' (Brannen, 1990, p.323).

Conclusion

Despite some reservations, *Adultery: An Analysis of Love and Betrayal* investigates an aspect of personal relationships that has so far been largely ignored. It attempts this by the increasingly popular, but still much debated, practice of combining quantitative and qualitative methods. Furthermore, as a result of its attempts to employ some degree of feminist evaluation of the material it serves to highlight a current paradox. That is, while there has been a '. . . convergence in thought and feeling between the two sexes that cannot be explained simply by suggesting women have learned to express themselves in similar ways to men . . . Yet there remain striking differences because for women the experience of adultery and divorce is different and much more serious than for men' (Lawson, 1988, p.288).

Bibliography and Further Reading

Atwater, L. (1982), *The Extramarital Connection: Sex, Intimacy and Identity*, New York, Irvington.

Atwater, L. (1990), Review of 'Adultery: an Analysis of Love and Betrayal' in *Journal of Marriage and the Family*, Vol.52, p.564.

Bhugra, D. (1989), Review of 'Adultery: An Analysis of Love and Betrayal' in *British Journal of Psychiatry*, Vol.155, p.875.

Brannen, J. (1990), Review of 'Adultery: An Analysis of Love and Betrayal' in *Sociology*, Vol.24 pp.323–4.

Drabelle, D. (1988), 'Marriage as a Myth' in *Psychology Today*, Vol.22, p.65.

Hunt, M. (1969), *The Affair: A Portrait of Extra-Marital Love in Contemporary America*, New York, World Publishing.

Lawson, A. (1988), *Adultery: An Analysis of Love and Betrayal*, Oxford, Basil Blackwell.

Oakley, A. (1989), 'Stolen Kisses' in *New Statesman and Society*, Vol.2, p.41.

Appendix

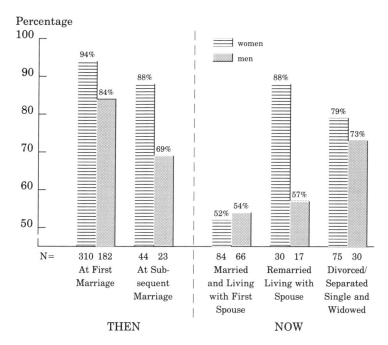

Figure 12.1 Belief in Fidelity for Self and Marital Career (Proportions saying they should be faithful).

THEN: At first marriage, both women and men believe strongly in sexual fidelity. If they divorce and re-marry, women (but fewer men) still believe in fidelity.

NOW: That is, in 1982–83 when completing the questionnaire – those still married to a first spouse believe in fidelity least, while remarried women but not remarried men, remain strongly committed to fidelity. The remainder of the sample who have not remarried occupy an intermediate position on fidelity.

(Lawson, 1988, Figure 2.1, p. 73)

13

Sexual Violence

Liz Kelly (1988), *Surviving Sexual Violence*, Oxford, Blackwell.

Wendy Langford

The Sociology of Sexual Violence

Sexual violence is a central fact of social life in contemporary Britain. It is likely that the vast majority of females, and some males will be subjected to some form of sexual violence at some point in their lives, often many times. Sexual violence takes many different forms, and might be seen to include behaviour such as rape, incest and sexual abuse, sexual harassment, 'flashing', sexual assault, etc. It occurs in the home, in public places, and in places of work and education. Sometimes men threaten or attack women they do not know, but often they do it to women they do know. Many women and girls are subjected to sexual violence by their own husbands, fathers, brothers, and boyfriends. As well as being directly hurt by sexual violence, the fact that it is so common makes women fearful and anxious about how they behave with men, and restricts their freedom in terms of where they can go, with whom, and at what times. The fear of sexual violence and the need to try and avoid it therefore affect the lives of all women.

Only a very small proportion of sexual violence is reported to the police or made public. People are generally aware only of those very few cases which reach the media, often because they involve somebody famous, or because the victim was killed during the attack. In most cases however, those assaulted are ordinary unknown people, who do survive the experience. Sociologists have become increasingly interested in trying to understand sexual violence. They have looked at such issues as how common it is; how it affects the lives of those who are subjected to it; how it is dealt with by the police and courts; and what it tells us about the nature of society, especially about relations between men and women, and between men and children.

The Study and Its Intellectual Context

Surviving Sexual Violence reports on 60 women's experiences of sexual violence. It considers how the women defined their experiences, and how they had been affected by what had happened to them. It also looks at what this information might tell us about relationships between women and men more generally, and what might have to change in society if sexual violence is to be ended or reduced.

The study forms part of a large body of sociological research about sexual violence which has been undertaken, particularly during the last 20 years. This work has included looking at particular aspects of sexual violence such as rape (Brownmiller, 1975), sexual harassment (Wise and Stanley, 1987), forced prostitution (Barry, 1979), incest and the sexual abuse of children (Nelson, 1987), wife beating (Dobash and Dobash, 1979), and rape within marriage (Russell, 1982). Some writers have looked at how women who report sexual violence are dealt with by the police, courts, and welfare agencies (Hanmer and Maynard, 1987). Others have investigated the relationship between sexual violence and sexuality (MacKinnon, 1987).

This research has helped to dispel much previous ignorance and mythology, and has produced a considerable amount of new information about the nature, extent, and effects of sexual violence. For example, it has been revealed that far from being a rare occurrence, all forms of sexual violence are much more common than was previously believed. It has also become apparent that the vast majority of sexual violence is carried out, not by psychologically disturbed men, but by men who are otherwise considered to be psychologically 'normal'. The old myth that men 'can't help it' has been shown to be false. Men choose to be violent, and much of the violence, whether directed at women they do not know or at their sisters, wives, mothers, girlfriends, colleagues, or children, is carefully planned in advance. It is also clear that sexual violence has much more widespread and significant effects on women and children than previously known, affecting them everywhere – in the home, the workplace, the school, and in public places. It is important to note that although attackers and abusers are almost always men, they do not always assault females. Many boys and some adult men are raped, assaulted and abused too. The law and state agencies fail to prevent or deal effectively with the majority of sexual violence. Most attackers and abusers are never brought to justice.

The more research that has been done on sexual violence, the more questions have been raised about it. Why is it so common? Why is it nearly always men who commit sexual violence? Why is so little done to stop it, or to help victims? How does sexual violence affect the lives of those who are subjected to it? What is the relationship between sexual violence and 'normal' sexual behaviour? What are the implications for relations between men and women and men and children? What can be done about sexual violence?

Surviving Sexual Violence builds on previous sociological research in three important respects. Firstly, it concentrates particularly on the experiences of women, looking at how they understand what has happened to them and how they define their experiences. Secondly, it is the first empirical study to report on the whole range of different forms of sexual violence experienced by women over their lifetimes, and to look at how these might be linked. Thirdly, the study looks at and emphasizes how women resist sexual violence, and how they develop strategies to cope with and survive the consequences of sexual violence. The study fits into traditions of sociological inquiry into *rape, sexuality, sexual violence, wife battering, incest and the sexual abuse of children, criminology,* and *gender relations.*

Research Design

Kelly's research sample was a voluntary one of 60 predominantly white British women with a considerable range with regard to age, class of origin, marital status, work experience and sexual identity. She interviewed three groups, each of ten women, who volunteered because they had experienced rape, incest, and domestic violence, respectively. Kelly also interviewed a comparison group of 30 other women, whose previous experience was unknown before they were interviewed. 47 of the total sample also gave a follow-up interview. In order to carry out successful interviews on a subject that is so painful and distressing, Kelly rejected a style of ' "objective" aloofness'. It was impossible to remain detached and yet enable women to trust her enough to talk about their experiences. As a result of a sympathetic interviewing style, women were able to talk in great depth about their experiences of sexual violence and about how it had affected their lives. This gave rich and interesting data.

Principal Findings

The study contributed to understanding sexual violence in three main areas: (i) definitions of sexual violence; (ii) the relationship of sexual violence to male dominance; and (iii) how women survive, cope with and resist the effects of sexual violence in their lives.

(i) *Definitions of sexual violence*

Perhaps the most important consideration about any study of sexual violence is how the subject is defined. The reasons why this is so are particularly highlighted by Kelly's research. For example, if women are asked whether they have been 'raped', and they say 'no', it might be assumed that therefore they had freely and happily consented to all the sexual experiences they have had. Kelly found however that this was certainly not the case. 28 (47%) of the respondents defined experiences they had had as rape (this figure is likely to be higher than average because ten of the 60 women defined themselves as having been raped) (Kelly, 1988, p. 88). However, many more of the women described experiences which they said were 'like rape' in that the man had put specific pressure on them to have sex, often involving the threat of, or actual, physical force (ibid., p. 84). Women were often very unsure whether to define their experiences as rape.

> I remember an occasion where he wouldn't let me get up, and he was very strong. He pulled my arms over my head. I didn't put up much of a *struggle*. I mean I wouldn't have seen that as rape because I associated rape with strangers, night and struggle. I didn't put up much of a struggle, but I *didn't want to*, so in a sense that was rape, yes.
>
> (ibid., p. 113)

In order to account for these experiences, Kelly introduced a new category – 'coercive sex'. 63% of the women in her study had experienced 'coercive sex', and 66% of those had experienced it more than once (ibid., p. 84). Moreover, even more women described experiences where although they had not said 'no', they felt pressured into having sex when they did not really want it – a phenomenon Kelly termed 'pressurized sex'.

> Where do you define rape? The pressure to have sex was so overwhelming . . . I was made to feel guilty. It wasn't rape, but *incredible* emotional pressure was put on and I wanted that man out of my room as soon as possible.'   (ibid., p. 112)
>   88% of the women in Kelly's sample had experienced pressurized sex. For 96% of these it was a repeated experience.   (ibid., p. 82)

This demonstrates that conventional definitions of heterosexual sex as being either 'rape' or 'not rape' are inadequate when it comes to understanding the experiences of women. The fact that women often feel threatened or pushed into having sex when they don't want to is important information which would not have come to light in a study which only counted 'rape' as being of interest, and used a narrow definition of what it was. Kelly's research is useful therefore in demonstrating that what researchers find out about sexual violence depends largely on what they count as being sexual violence in the first place.

(ii) *The relationship of sexual violence to male dominance*

Kelly used a definition of sexual violence which covered 'any physical, visual, verbal, or sexual act that is experienced by the woman or girl, at the time or later, as a threat, invasion or assault, that has the effect of hurting her or degrading her and/or takes away her ability to control intimate contact' (ibid., p.41). This is a wider definition than many other researchers have used. The advantage is that, as we have seen, this enabled Kelly to investigate how women actually experienced such encounters, thus producing important new information about sexual violence. It showed that in reality, what is or is not 'violent' is not as obvious as people might think. There was found to be no clear boundary between what might be considered 'normal' everyday male behaviour and 'aberrant' male behaviour – they in fact 'shade into' one another (ibid., p.75). For example some people might consider it 'normal' behaviour for men to try and 'persuade' a woman to have sex, when she is reluctant. The woman's experience might be that this was an aggressive and deeply distressing experience.

For this reason, Kelly argues that sexual violence is best understood as a 'continuum of prevalence'. By this she means that the whole range of different forms of sexual violence can be linked together by arranging them in a line or 'continuum' according to how often women experience them in their lives. At one end are women's everyday experiences of threat or fear of violence, ranging through sexual harassment, pressurized sex, sexual assault, obscene phone calls, coercive sex, domestic violence, sexual abuse, and flashing, to the comparatively less frequent experiences of rape and incest at the other (see *Table 13.1*, p.129). It is important to realize that it is not a continuum of seriousness, as this is hard to measure in this way. Sometimes women can be deeply distressed and frightened by incidents which others might see as relatively less serious.

Kelly's concept of the continuum of sexual violence is useful because it shows the range and extent of sexual violence which occurs throughout women's lives. This demonstrates that sexual violence is not simply a deviant activity involving a few men and a few unlucky women. On the contrary, it shows that although some women suffer more extremely than others, sexual violence in one form or another is a more or less common feature of all women's lives. It also shows that although there may be many men who never abuse, assault, or threaten women and children, very large numbers of men do. Kelly's results confirm those of many previous studies in suggesting that sexual violence is an important way in which male dominance in society is maintained. This is illustrated by what she found out about the effects it has on women, individually and as a social group.

(iii) *The effects of sexual violence on women's lives*

The women in Kelly's study reported a wide range of consequences of their experiences of sexual violence. One of the most common was an inability to feel safe or secure on the streets, or in the company of men – sometimes even in their own homes. Many women's feelings about sexuality were affected so that they were unable to enjoy sex because of feeling used, dirty, or being unable to relax. Many women internalized the way that women are often blamed for men's violence, and blamed themselves for what had happened to them, even though there was no 'logical' reason to do so. Many women felt ashamed and bad about themselves because of what had happened to them so that it affected their self-confidence. Women who had been sexually abused as girls reported growing up with a sense of fear and threat, having nightmares and problems with their schooling. Some women had been so affected by experiences of sexual violence that they suffered severe depression, had nervous breakdowns, or attempted suicide.

The fact that sexual violence is such a widespread practice also has considerable implications for women as a social group. For example, the threat of possible violence places severe restrictions on women's social mobility outside their homes, determining where they can go, by which route, by which method of transport, who with, and at which times of the day. For many women and girls, as well as many boys, the home itself is not a safe place because they are subjected to sexual abuse from other family members, as well as threatening behaviour from outside, such as obscene 'phone calls'. Workplaces and educational establishments are also places where women and girls are subjected to sexual harassment, assault and threats. Kelly found that *none* of her 60 respondents was able to feel safe at all times and all places from the threat of sexual violence (ibid., p.79).

Sexual violence and the threat of it also place great restrictions on women's interractions with men so that their subordination is reinforced in other ways. For example, a women who has been raped or battered by her husband is likely to become afraid of him so that she is unable to express her feelings, or assert herself in the relationship.

> I would just be quite passive, try not to provoke him verbally or physically. I would just do anything he wanted me to, try and be calm and pleasant just to try and avoid it or if there was a warning I would flee the house.   (ibid., p.180)

Similarly, women who are sexually harassed in the workplace may put up with it, for fear that if they complain they might get worse harassment, or if the man is in a higher position than them, they may fear losing their job. The chance for women to develop their own autonomous sexuality is also restricted. Being 'persuaded' or pressurised into sex leaves little room for women and girls to decide if, when, where, with whom, or in what ways, *they* wish to express their sexuality. All in all, women's full and equal participation in society is considerably undermined by the practice of sexual violence.

Despite this huge impact on women's lives, Kelly is critical of the idea that women and girls are just helpless 'victims' of sexual violence. She found that women had used a wide variety of means to resist and survive assaults. Some had managed to successfully fight off an attacker. Others had cut their feelings off from the experience to protect themselves, although this strategy could in itself cause psychological problems. Some had managed to leave violent partners and start a new life, despite tremendous problems. Women often reported that even though their experiences had been very painful, they had managed to learn things which were useful and had helped them to survive.

Kelly points out however that women's strategies for surviving and resisting sexual violence have often wrongly been seen as a problem. For example, one of the most common things women learned from their experiences was not to trust men (ibid., p.221). This has sometimes been seen as a problem that women should learn to overcome. Kelly disagrees, stressing that trusting men too easily in such a sexually violent society is in fact very dangerous for women and children. She therefore concludes that 'women's distrust of men might be a rational and self protective response' (ibid., p.202). For many women, their experiences had taught them about the reality of the power imbalance between the sexes.

> It just opened my eyes to so much of what happens between men and women. I suppose to the fact that I never really had any pleasure out of sex, the double standards . . . in the long term it's had very dramatic effects.   (ibid., p.224)

Asked what they thought caused sexual violence in society, most of the respondents cited men's attitudes to women and sex, and male power and dominance. This can be seen from *Table 13.2*, p.130.

Despite the trauma they had been caused by being subject to sexual violence, Kelly continually found that the women she interviewed displayed remarkable courage in the ways they had managed to resist, survive, cope with, and learn from their experiences. She therefore prefers to use the term 'survivor' rather than the more common term 'victim', which can imply that women are passive and helpless. Kelly found that a major factor in how well women were able to cope and survive was how they were able to define their experience. Women in society are often blamed for violence inflicted upon them and can therefore feel that it was their own fault. Having their experiences seen for what they are and taken seriously is important and empowering for women. Many of the women felt that taking part in the research had itself helped them to come to terms with what had happened to them. Kelly believes that understanding how women survive, cope with and resist sexual violence is important to being able to work towards ending it. Also interesting are the the women's views on how sexual violence might be prevented (see *Table 13.3*, p.130).

Critical Observations

Surviving Sexual Violence provides a unique insight into women's experiences of the variety and frequency of different forms of sexual violence to which they are subjected by men, both as adults and as children, and of how this is linked to women's subordinate status in society and their efforts to resist male dominance. The study has generally been praised for its contribution to many areas of sociology. It has also recieved some criticisms.

One concern was that because Kelly's sample was not a representative sample of society, her statistics are not particularly useful (Wiliams, 1990, p.425). This is because Kelly's research is 'qualitative' research. Her aim was to find out what was interesting about the experiences of the particular women she studied, and what they could tell us about sexual violence. This means that Kelly's statistics are useful in exploring the concept of the continuum of prevalence and the attitudes and beliefs of her respondents about sexual violence. However, the sample was not meant to be statistically representative of the population as a whole. It remains to be seen therefore, whether a large scale quantitative study would produce a similar 'continuum of prevalence' to Kelly's. In the meantime, the statistical incidence of different forms of sexual violence has been documented by other researchers (Baker, 1983; Hall, 1985).

Williams also considers that as the great strength of Kelly's work is that it helps us to understand what experiencing sexual violence is actually like for women and how it affects their lives, she should have included more informaton about the women's lives in her book and more actual quotes from the interviews (Williams, 1990, p.425). She recognizes that Kelly might have been constrained by her wish to protect the anonymity of the women, but feels that we miss out on 'a great fund of qualitative information'.

A third criticism is that although Kelly herself is attentive to the importance of naming forms of sexual violence so that they can be seen for what they are (e.g. coercive sex, pressurized sex), she uses the neutral term 'domestic violence' to describe assaults in the home. Holmstrom (1990, p.1120) considers that this disguises the fact that the violence is inflicted by men on women and would consider the term 'wife abuse' to be more accurate.

Conclusion

By concentrating on how women actually experience sexual violence, *Surviving Sexual Violence* provides a systematic account of how the many different types of violence and intimidation to which women are subjected by men are linked. The results confirm the work of many other sociologists who have argued that sexual violence is a primary means by which women's subordination in society is ensured. The study indicates therefore that recognizing the prevalence and effects of sexual violence and resisting it both individually and collectively is important for anyone who is concerned about the position and well-being of women and children in society.

Bibliography and Further Reading

Adler, E.S. (1991), Review of 'Surviving Sexual Violence' in *Gender and Society*, Vol. 5, No. 4, pp. 624–628.

Baker, T. (1983), 'Readers Survey on Sexual Abuse' in *19 Magazine*, Sept.

Barry, K. (1979), *Female Sexual Slavery*, New Jersey, Prentice Hall.

Brownmiller, S. (1975), *Against Our Will: Men, Women and Rape*, New York, Simon and Schuster.

Dobash, R. and Dobash, R. (1979), *Violence Against Wives: A Case Against the Patriarchy*, New York, Free Press.

Hall, R. (1985), *Ask Any Woman*, Bristol, Falling Wall.

Holstrom, L.L. (1990), Review of 'Surviving Sexual Violence' in *American Journal of Sociology*, Vol. 95, No. 4, pp.1119–1121.

Hanmer, J. and Maynard, M. (eds.) (1987), *Women, Violence and Social Control*, London, Macmillan.

Kelly, L. (1988), *Surviving Sexual Violence*, Oxford, Blackwell.

MacKinnon, C. (1987), *Feminism Unmodified*, Harvard University Press.

Nelson, S. (1987), *Incest: Fact and Myth*, Edinburgh, Stramullion.

Russell, D. (1982), *Rape in Marriage*, New York, MacMillan.

Stanko, E. (1985), *Intimate Intrusions: Women's Experience of Male Violence*, London, Routledge.

Williams, L.M. (1990), Review of 'Surviving Sexual Violence' in *Contemporary Sociology*, Vol. 19, pp. 424–426.

Wise, S. and Stanley, L. (1987), *Sexual Harassment in Everyday Life*, London, Pandora.

Appendices

Table 13.1 The continuum of prevalence

Form of violence	Number of women	%of sample
Threat of violence	60	100
Sexual harassment	56	93
Pressure to have sex	50	83
Sexual assault	42	70
Obscene phone calls[a]	25	68 (of 37)
Coercive sex	38	63
Domestic violence[b]	32	53
Sexual abuse	30	50
Flashing	30	50
Rape[b]	30	50
Incest[b]	13	22

[a] This category was added when a woman noted its absence; 23 interviews and follow-ups had already been completed.

[b] These 3 categories include 10 women (17 per cent) who identified themselves as having had these experiences before the interviews.

(Kelly, 1988, Table 4.1, p. 78)

Table 13.2 Why rape, domestic violence and incest occur

	R		I		DV		C1		Total[a]	
	N	%	N	%	N	%	N	%	N	%
Men's attitudes to women	5	50	7	70	6	60	8	53	26	58
Men's attitudes to sex	4	40	6	60	1	10	6	40	17	38
Male dominance	5	50	1	10	3	30	2	13	11	24
Relationships based on power	3	30	0	0	2	20	4	27	9	20
Men are allowed to be violent	2	20	3	30	1	10	1	17	7	16
Stress	0	0	0	0	2	20	3	20	5	11
Women seen by men as property	0	0	1	10	3	30	0	0	4	9
Violent individuals	0	0	1	10	1	10	2	13	4	9
Alcohol	0	0	0	0	1	10	1	7	2	4

[a] Women gave more than one answer. Percentages calculated on number of women in subgroup R, I and DV = 10, C1 = 15, Total = 45.   (ibid., Table 9.3, p. 229)

Table 13.3 How can sexual violence be prevented?

	R		I		DV		C1		C2		Total[a]	
	N	%	N	%	N	%	N	%	N	%	N	%
Change men	9	90	4	40	2	20	5	33	5	33	25	42
Change whole society/family structure	4	40	2	20	4	40	6	40	9	60	24	40
Make women stronger	2	20	0	0	4	40	4	27	6	40	16	27
Educate women and children	1	10	2	20	4	40	2	13	4	27	13	22
Punish men	3	30	1	10	1	10	0	0	1	7	6	10
Earlier intervention	0	0	0	0	2	20	1	7	2	13	5	8

[a] More than one answer possible. Percentages calculated on the same basis as in Table 13.2.   (ibid., Table 9.4, p. 230)

R = group (10) who defined themselves prior to the study as survivors of rape.
I = group (10) who defined themselves prior to the study as survivors of incest.
DV = group (10) who defined themselves prior to the study as survivors of domestic violence.
C1 and C2 = two control groups of fifteen women each.

14

Lone Parents and Poverty

Jane Millar (1989), *Poverty and the Lone-parent Family: the challenge of social policy*, Aldershot, Avebury.

Anne Witz

The Lone-parent Family

Lone-parent families are far more numerous now than they used to be and currently make up about 13% of all families with children in Britain. 90% of lone-parents are women. The main problem facing lone-mothers is how to provide financial and caring support simultaneously in a society which is still organized around the assumption that families are nuclear units with a gendered division of labour, where the male parent is the main breadwinner and the female parent is the main child-carer and houseworker. Lone-parent families face a very high risk of poverty, which presents a challenge to social policy.

Poverty and the Lone-parent Family is an empirical study of the incomes and living standards of poor lone-parent families in Britain. It provides a detailed analysis of sources of income and patterns of expenditure, evaluates income support policy towards such families and recommends ways in which social policy could develop in the future. In particular, it demonstrates the gap between policy provision and the needs of lone-parent families. In addition, policy provision in Britain is compared to that in other countries: EC countries, Nordic countries, Australia, Canada and the United States.

It is vital that sociologists locate analyses of lone-parent families within other aspects of contemporary British society. There are clear links between the social and economic situation in which lone-parent families find themselves and gender inequalities in society. Most lone-parent families are headed by women. *Gender segregation in employment*, especially women's concentration in low-paid, part-time and insecure jobs, means that lone-mothers are extremely vulnerable to poverty. The lone-parent family is also a manifestation of *changing* family structure, as two thirds of lone-parent families are a result of marital breakdown. There is a clear link, then, between rising divorce rates and increasing numbers of lone-parent families. In due course, the lone-parent family may become a two-parent one, which is a re-constituted family. Studying lone-parent families fits into sociological debates about *poverty*, the *family*, *divorce* and, most importantly, *gender divisions* in contemporary British society.

Research Design

Millar's study of lone-parent families is based on secondary analysis of two data-sets: the Family Finances Survey (FFS) and the Family Resources Survey (FRS). Secondary analysis is a method whereby data collected by someone else, often for a different purpose, is subjected to re-examination. Both studies were originally carried out by the Office of Population Census and Surveys for the Department of Health and Social Security between 1978 and 1980. The FFS survey was designed to be a replication of the Family Expenditure Survey (FES), which is a representative sample of all households and gives detailed information about household income and expenditure. The number of low-income families included in the FES sample is too small to enable any detailed analysis, and so the FFS was designed to be a FES for low-income families.

Low-income families were defined as those with net incomes of less than 140% of supplementary benefit level. The sample consisted of 3,000 low-income, lone-parent and two-parent families with dependent children. Data collection methods in the FFS involved (a) asking families to keep a two-week diary of expenditure and (b) interviewing, using the same questionnaire as that used in the FES. The FFS was followed by another survey, the FRS, in order to see how long families remained on low incomes and so provided a longitudinal element, or picture over time. All families were re-interviewed a year later, but this time they were not asked to keep expenditure diaries.

Secondary analysis of the FFS and FRS data-sets by Millar yielded very detailed information of income (earnings, benefits and maintenance) and living standards (indicated by patterns of expenditure, access to assets and savings and debts). It also provided information on movements in and out of poverty, because income levels at the time of the second, FRS interview could be compared with those at the first, FFS interview.

In addition to re-analysing existing data sets, Millar drew upon secondary sources, as distinct from secondary analysis, to compare the situation of lone-parent families in different countries and examine whether this was eased or exacerbated by different forms of policy provision. This provided a comparative perspective on lone-parent families.

Principal Findings

The study concentrated on three main issues: incomes and living standards; dependence on the state; and the persistence of poverty. It also compared the situation of poor lone-parent families in Britain with those in other countries.

(i) *Incomes and living standards*

Millar looked at the relative contribution of earnings, benefits, maintenance and other incomes (mainly pensions and investments) to the gross weekly earnings of lone-parent families and compared this to two-parent families. Sources of income were very different for two-parent and lone-parent families. Lone-parent families were twice as likely as two-parent ones to depend mainly on social security benefits. The types of social security benefit received were also different. 69% of lone-mothers relied on supplementary benefit as their main source of income, compared to only 18% of two-parent families. But, whereas 11% of two-parent families relied on unemployment benefit as their main source of income, none of the lone-parents did.

To get a clearer picture of living standards it is better to look at net, or disposable, incomes. This was defined by Millar as gross income less tax, national insurance contributions, housing costs and work expenses. Because larger families tend to have higher net incomes (most receive child-benefit which is not taxed and which increases with more children), Millar controlled for differences in family size. She found that low-income families in employment were the best off, whilst those on supplementary benefit were the worst off. Among the lone-mothers, the poorest were young women with young children, living in rented accommodation and solely dependent on supplementary benefit. The better off were older women with older children who were more likely to have incomes from sources other than, or in addition to, supplementary benefit (such as earnings, widows benefits or maintenance).

How low incomes translate into low living standards was measured by expenditure and access to consumer assets. *Table 14.1*, p. 138 shows that the largest proportion of lone-mothers' total expenditure (just under one third) went on food, followed by housing costs (21%) and then fuel (11.5%). Lone-mothers and two-parent families spent most of their money on basic essentials; but this was particularly true for lone-mothers, for whom about two-thirds of total expenditure was on essentials. *Table 14.2*, p.138 shows that lone-mothers' access to consumer goods is predictably low, relative to other families with children. They are equally as likely to have televisions, only slightly less likely to have washing machines, fridge-feezers and central-heating, but are much less likely to have access to cars and telephones, which means they may be more socially isolated than two-parent families.

(ii) *Dependence on the state*

Millar found that state benefits were a major source of income for lone-parents, which means that lone-parents are a social group which is highly dependent on state welfare. Millar discusses this welfare dependency from two perspectives. The first is state support for working families who do not receive supplementary benefit but do have incomes. For these families both child-benefit and means-tested benefit provide valuable support, but particularly child-benefit because it is taken up by almost everyone eligible. The second perspective assesses the extent of welfare dependency by lone-parent families in receipt of supplementary benefit. For lone-mothers, most of whom will not be in employment, supplementary benefit was of the greatest importance, and provided a continuing source of income on which they were dependent for several years.

Is there a 'dependency culture' amongst lone-mothers? Millar finds that a substantial proportion of lone-mothers moved on and off benefit, which suggests caution regarding the concept of a 'dependency culture'. However, only 17% of the lone-mothers in the sample were never on benefit during the period of the study so, more than other types of low-income family (lone-fathers and two-parent families), lone-mothers were most likely to be continuously on benefit. They escaped poverty either by finding a husband or by finding a job. The most likely route was by finding a husband and becoming 'ex-lone-mothers', unless they ended up living with an unemployed or low-paid man. So it was changes in marital, rather than employment status that took mothers on and off benefit, and therefore in and out of poverty. Of the lone-mothers who (re)married (or who were co-habiting) the vast majority came off supplementary benefit. By contrast, it was changes in employment status that were crucial in determining the movement in and out of poverty for two-parent families.

(iii) *The persistence of poverty*

Turning to the issue of the persistence of poverty, Millar's findings provide support for the notion of a *poverty trap* for lone-parent families. She was able to look at movements in and out of poverty by comparing changes in incomes of families between the first (FFS) and the second (FRS) interview one year later. 'Escape' from poverty was defined as a rise in income relative to supplementary benefit of at least 20 percentage points.

Although about a quarter of low-income families escaped from poverty during the 12 months covered by the two surveys, nonetheless two-parent families has a greater chance of escaping poverty than lone-parents. In particular, to remain a lone-mother was to remain in poverty, whilst to marry or re-marry usually meant escaping poverty.

For lone-mothers dependent on state benefit, then, the main impression conveyed by Millar is of a life characterized by financial hardship and a very restricted life-style. If the choice is between long-term dependence on the low income provided by supplementary benefit or short-term dependence interspersed with spells in what will most probably be low-paid employment, then neither of these options seemed to provide lone-mothers and their children with an adequate standard of living. Marriage, it seems, offers lone-mothers the most likely escape from a life of poverty.

(iv) *Comparative data: Britain and other countries*

Millar compares different sources of income of lone-parents in various countries and evaluates the success of different forms of state provision in maintaining the relative living standards of lone-mothers (relative, that is, to a country's own living standard).

In most countries lone-mothers and children have an above average risk of being in poverty, with Sweden being the main exception. One of the most crucial differences between countries is an ideological one, which relates to whether or not it is considered appropriate for lone-mothers to be in paid employment. In the UK and Australia the ideology of domesticity for women is reinforced by social security benefits being provided as a *replacement* for earnings. In other European countries, the Nordic countries and the United States, lone-mothers' labour market participation is facilitated by benefits acting as a *supplement* to earnings. The outcome of this can be seen in the different labour market participation rates of lone-mothers across the different countries, and *Table 14.3*, p.139 shows that only 39% of lone-mothers worked in the UK, compared to 69% in France and 86% in Sweden.

Discussion

Poverty and the Lone-parent Family provides solid documentation of how lone-mothers are particularly vulnerable to poverty in society. It provides further substantive evidence for feminist arguments that the British welfare state enforces female dependency on a male breadwinner; as Millar demonstrates, lone-mothers' main escape route from poverty is by becoming 'ex-lone-mothers' through marriage or cohabitation with a man. For lone-mothers, taking paid employment does not keep poverty at bay to the same extent as marriage or cohabitation.

The policy implications of Millar's study are complex, and remain a controversial topic of political debate. Should income support policy for lone-parents be based primarily on the principle of state support, or private maintenance (e.g. through support by the absent partner), or self-support through employment? Millar argues that what we currently have is not an income support policy specifically geared towards meeting the needs of lone-parent families, but only a series of additions to existing provisions which are designed primarily to meet the needs of two-parent families. In addition, the 'family' is assumed to consist of a male breadwinner, a female carer and their own dependent children. These prescribed roles for men and women are assumed to continue even when the two-parent 'family' no longer exists, with the result that a double standard operates: it is assumed that lone-fathers should continue to be financial providers, but that lone-mothers should continue to be carers. It is precisely this chain of assumptions underlying income support policy for families that is the primary cause of the particularly high risk of poverty among lone-mothers. This leads Millar to insist that, for lone-mothers, it is their sex rather than their marital status which is the real key to understanding why they are poor. Ultimately, then, Millar's explanation of the high risk of poverty faced by lone-mothers compared to lone-fathers is in terms of gender divisions in contemporary society, particularly the ideology of domesticity for women and the way in which this shapes policy provision. This, in turn, leads Millar to place great emphasis on the links between gender and poverty.

Millar's research contributes to a sociological understanding of the relationship between poverty and gender, particularly in terms of seeing poverty amongst women, in this case lone-mothers, as a structural, rather than an individual problem. It alerts us to the urgent need to make visible the gendered dimensions of poverty. Mack and Lansley's (1985) conclusion that 'women are not significantly more at risk of poverty than men' is highly questionable, particularly as they recognize that the majority of lone-parents are women. An issue that awaits further clarification is whether the so-called 'feminization of poverty' is a recent social trend or whether it is an artefact, produced by the use of more gender-sensitive measures of poverty. It is partly the case that sociological research has obscured female poverty because of the way poverty has traditionally been measured and defined. For example, treating the family or household as an aggregate unit obscures the unequal distribution of resources between men and women within these units (Graham, 1984). However, it would be incautious to conclude that the increased visibility of women's poverty is simply the result of using more gender-sensitive measures of poverty. Demographic shifts have meant, for example, that lone elderly women are increasing in number, and often living in poverty. There is also a very real sense in which women's poverty is increasing for, if we live in a society where more and more people are living in poverty, then – precisely because of the links between gender and poverty – women will be disproportionately represented in the swelling ranks of the poor (Millar, 1989; Glendinning and Millar, 1987).

As regards the methodology used in Millar's study, there are always disadvantages to secondary analysis. In this case, as Millar herself recognizes, there were omissions from the data (on low income rather than lone-parent families) which would have been included if the survey had been designed specifically to investigate lone-parent families. For example, there were no questions about marital status, which meant that lone-parents were not asked whether they were single, widowed, divorced or separated, how long they had been lone-parents, or whether they received maintenance payment. The FFS/FRS also included very few lone-fathers, which in one sense is not surprising given that they are less likely to be poor than lone-mothers. This means, however, that Millar's study focusses on lone-mothers rather than lone-fathers.

Research into the social and economic circumstances of lone-parents is, in effect, research into the nature and causes of gender inequalities, precisely because lone-parents are disproportionately female. Further research by Popay and Jones (1990) provides insights into the quality of life of lone-mothers by examining the subjective experience of health and illness amongst lone-parents, compared to two-parent families. They show how poverty takes a considerable toll on lone-mothers' health and find that the adverse health effects associated with caring work in the home are greater, the poorer the material circumstances in which this is done. Lone-mothers, then, face greater health risks than other women, because of their greater likelihood of living in poverty, whilst the social isolation they experience can also lead to poor mental health.

The topic of poor one-parent families, and in particular the fact that these are predominantly female-headed, highlights the importance of investigating the relation between gender and poverty more generally, particularly the relation between women's paid work and poverty, women's poverty and welfare, and women's poverty in the family (Glendinning and Millar, 1987).

Bibliography and Further Reading

Glendinning, C. and Millar, J. (eds.) (1987), *Women and Poverty in Britain*, Brighton, Wheatsheaf Books.

Glendinning, C. and Millar, J. (1991), 'Poverty: the forgotten English-woman: reconstructing research and policy on poverty' in Mavis Maclean and Dulcie Groves (eds.), *Women's Issues in Social Policy*, London, Routledge.

Graham, H. (1984), *Women, Health and the Family*, London, Harvester Wheatsheaf.

Mack, J. and Lansley, S. (1985), *Poor Britain*, London, Allen and Unwin.

Millar, J. (1989), 'Social security, equality and women in the UK' in *Policy and Politics*, Vol.17, No.4, pp.311–319.

Millar, J. and Glendenning, C. (1989), 'Gender and Poverty' in *Journal of Social Policy*, Vol.18, No.3, pp.363–83.

Popay, J. and Jones, G. (1990), 'Patterns of health and illness amongst lone parents' in *Journal of Social Policy*, Vol.19, No.4, pp.499–534.

Appendices

Table 14.1 Expenditure on main commodity groups by family type: single-unit households

	As a proportion of total expenditure	
Commodity	Lone mothers %	Two-parent families %
Food	31.5	31.4
Housing	21.4	16.7
Transport	4.0	9.6
Fuel	11.5	9.2
Clothing and footwear	7.2	6.2
Services	6.6	6.2
Durables	4.5	5.0
Other household goods	7.4	6.9
Tobacco	4.1	5.0
Alcohol	0.7	2.7
Miscellaneous	1.2	0.9
Total	100	100
Base (number interviewed)	754	1307
	(835)	(1688)

(Millar, 1989, Table 4.16, p. 75)

Table 14.2 Access to consumer assets by family type: single-unit households

	FFS families		All families[1] with children (FES)	
Proportion with:	Lone mothers %	Two-parent families %	Lone parents %	Two-parent families %
Telephone	39	50	62	74
Television	97	97	95	98
Washing machine	69	84	81	94
Fridge/freezer	88	92	95	98
Car	9	52	28	76
Central heating	45	47	55	65
Base (number interviewed)	754 (835)	1307 (1688)	233	937

[1] Family Expenditure Survey 1979, Table 5.
(ibid., Table 4.17, p. 76)

Table 14.3 Proportions in employment, lone mothers and married mothers: various countries

Country	Proportions in employment		Of those employed, proportion in full-time jobs[1]	
	Lone mothers	Married mothers	Lone mothers	Married mothers
Australia (1985)	35	47	59	43
Canada (1979)	63	58	–	–
Denmark (1978)[2]	89	79	64	40
France (1979)	69	41	–	–
FR Germany (1982)	60	42	63	42
Sweden (1979)	86	64	–	–
UK (1982/84)	39	49	44	29
US (1980)	71	60	80	64

[1] Definitions of full-time vary, but at least over 30 hours in all cases.
[2] Those with two children only, includes employed and registered unemployed.
(ibid., Table 7.2, p. 139)

15

Families, Communities and Health

Jocelyn Cornwell (1984), *Hard-Earned Lives*, London, Tavistock.

Sandie Lawrinson

Introduction

Carried out in Bethnall Green, the same area of London as Young and Willmott's (1957), *Family and Kinship in East London*, this fluent study concentrates on the 'commonsense' ideas held by a small group of working class people with regard to health and illness, and explores the ways in which these ideas can be situated in the wider contexts of their lives.

At some point in our lives we all have to confront issues of health and illness, either in ourselves or in people close to us. This means that we all have feelings about health at a commonsense level; about how to maintain good health; about how to deal with illness and about the place of professional health care provision within our lives. This examination of health issues both indicates and reinforces the idea that women are the primary carers in terms of family health. Gender divisions are manifested when women are usually the ones who provide the diet that hopefully keeps their family healthy; they are the ones who deal most commonly with minor ailments such as colds and influenza; and it is women in the main who seek professional medical care for family members who have more serious medical conditions.

Three major themes emerge from the book. First, the author distinguishes between the 'public' and the 'private' accounts she was able to collect from the people she interviewed. 'Public' accounts, she states, make interviewees feel more secure. They are provided in the context of question and answer encounters where the agenda is set by the interviewer, and are a response to the unfamiliar situation of being interviewed. In such situations it is culturally normal to maintain some social distance and present oneself in the best light possible to the researcher who is, by virtue of her education and experience, socially distanced from the interviewee. 'Private' accounts, on the other hand, occur when people are not asked to answer questions but are asked to recount details of their lives almost as stories. Usually these accounts are described as they would be to people who were socially closer to the interviewee; who would be likely to know and understand precisely what was being described. The attention of the interviewee, in this context, is focused more on the tale being told than on the fact that they are in the unfamiliar situation of being interviewed. In this way, the agenda is set less by the researcher and more by the person being researched. The author suggests that people can shift from 'public' to 'private' accounts within the same interview.

Second, the book is about the place of medicine and medical care in the lives of ordinary people. The author illustrates the ways in which perceptions of health and illness are sometimes linked to codes of behaviour that are deemed to be morally acceptable or unacceptable. In addition, the study documents gender differences in relation to the take-up of professional medical care services.

Third, the book is, in part, about the value of community life and the sense of solidarity experienced by inhabitants previously documented in other community studies (see, for example, Bell and Newby, 1972 and Young and Wilmott, 1957). It depicts community opposition to change and draws on the work of Marris (1974) to illustrate the sense of loss felt by residents when slum clearance breaks up long established neighbourhoods.

Research Design

Cornwell describes her research method as a 'case study which attempts to give a theoretical as well as a descriptive account of its case material' (Cornwell, 1984, p.1). Data were drawn from a variety of networks within Bethnall Green and the book is based largely on the information provided by 24 individuals who lived on the same estate. Many of them were related, or were friends or neighbours, and others were members of the local Residents' Association and were known to each other. The study provides a wealth of detail that goes beyond health perception and incorporates many issues related to social networks.

The sample used could not be said to be representative in a statistical sense, but was judged to be 'typical', in a more generally accepted way, of people whose 'lives faithfully reflect the history of social and economic life in East London over the past eighty or more years' (ibid., p.1). The locality in which the study took place has been subject to many changes over the last 60 years. Terrible pre-war housing conditions and the effects of the Blitz resulted in slum clearance and re-housing projects that caused family and social networks to be 'formed and re-formed'. Despite this, similarities between the interviewees and past generations remain; the men and women in the sample are employed locally, as were previous generations; and perception and use of health-care facilities are tied to the particular services available in the area.

The research was conducted in three stages. The first, a pilot study, involved four women and two men from three households who were all known to each other. The second stage involved six women and one man from six households that were part of the same extended family. These two stages had relied on gaining interviewees from the same social networks. This strategy was abandoned for the third and final stage when it was acknowledged that the concept 'social network' was not as useful as had initially been thought. Working within social networks was helpful in bringing about introductions and thereby facilitating access to would-be interviewees, but it held less value in the context of a study on medicine and medical services. The author had found that discussions about these issues were not carried out throughout the whole network but within small pockets of it. Moreover, the networks themselves were held together largely by the relationships of the women within them, making them less of a large social network and more of a series of relationships between women. It was felt necessary to incorporate the perceptions of more men but the women from the first two stages had been reluctant to recruit their menfolk. A visit to the local Residents' Association meeting provided access to four more households in which six men and five women agreed to participate. Data were collected in the homes of the interviewees. A total of 70 hours of interviews were tape-recorded and supplemented by field notes from a further 60 hours of contact and observation. Working on the assumption that people's perceptions of health issues are related to their way of life, and in order to put interviewee's perceptions about health into the wider context of their lives, the research covered other issues such as housing, education, employment and family history.

Principal Findings

The study set out to provide a rounded examination of people's lives while paying particular attention to perceptions of health and illness. As a result the findings cover issues related to (i) housing, (ii) work and family life, as well as (iii) health and illness.

(i) *Housing*

Changes in housing provision in the location of the study is reflected in the housing experiences of the sample. Older members recall the overcrowding and difficult living conditions of their childhood pre-war days when often two or more households lived together in one house. The onset of the second world war meant some of the children in the area were evacuated to safer places for the duration of the war. However, many parents refused to be separated from their children, and others soon brought their evacuated children back to London to be with them. House moves were common, households were disrupted and education discontinuous.

Post-war over-crowding was worse than ever because so many homes had been destroyed and, with one or two exceptions, all the sample began their married lives living with parents. Subsequent slum clearance and re-housing projects brought other problems in their wake. The new housing provided was not in the same locality and, despite vastly improved living conditions, some people objected to being re-housed because they were attached to the area and to their lives and relationships within it, and because they objected to other people making decisions about where they should live. Some moved away only to return when the opportunity arose.

An important feature of the data on housing is what it tells us about the community in which the housing was set and the sample lived, and the way in which accounts of the community are separated into 'public' and 'private' accounts; each telling a different story. To illustrate this point the author refers to the earlier works of Young and Willmott (1957) in which they paint a picture of Bethnal Green as a community with a valued collective life for its members who also enjoyed the privacy of their own homes. Their subsequent study of the same area (1971) suggested that the collective life of the community was actually more important to its members than their privacy. Inhabitants of Bethnal Green were portrayed as 'human' and caring of each other's well-being. This image of Bethnal Greeners is the image that came across to the author in the 'public' accounts of their community life and she provides a variety of telling quotations that confirm this image.

On the other hand, the 'private' accounts presented Bethnal Green residents in a very different light. In these the inhabitants showed themselves to be more self-centred than Young and Willmott ever suggested. Moreover, there were clear distinctions between the way that men and women, the old and the young, and people of different employment status' experienced community life. Using quotations from men and women living in the same household the author demonstrates that not only is the perception of men and women different with regard to the community, but that neither are able to provide a full account of what community life is like. For example:

> Mick Chalmers: 'I mean you can walk down here in the daytime and you don't even see a soul. I mean I don't know who lives two doors away from me'.
> Sarah Chalmers: 'See, what it is, with Mick it's different, but with me, I can walk outside the door, walk around the shops where it would take five minutes to walk there and back, and I'll be out half an hour, three-quarters of an hour. Because I bump into people that I know and talk and everything else.' (ibid., p. 50)

This raises questions not only about the concept of 'community' but also about the worth of Young and Willmott's somewhat romantic depiction of community which appear to be premised on 'public' discourse only (Lock, 1986, p.594).

(ii) *Work and family life*

Employment means very different things to the men and the women in the sample. Men were more preoccupied with paid labour outside of the home, women with domestic labour within it, which dictated their relationship to employment in the sexually segregated labour market of east London. This dichotomy is considered to be 'normal'. People's perception of normality becomes very important in the context of discussions about health matters because illness is seen to be 'abnormal' for two reasons: firstly, illness is a condition that interrupts 'normality'; secondly, illness is itself abnormal, being neither usual nor expected. It is useful to get a general understanding of what people consider to be usual and expected. Data on work and the family provides this, as well as offering a base onto which perceptions of health issues can be grounded.

Though the men interviewed had varied experiences of paid work, all but one were employed in jobs traditionally found in the area. The women, again with one exception, had experienced interruptions to their paid working lives when they left work to have children, returning only once the children had started school. 'Public' accounts showed that the sample considered 'you are what you are meant to be'. This was the same for both women and men, and for people with varying levels of intelligence, thus rationalizing differences in employment status. At the same time, the idea that 'life is what you make it' also emerged. This suggests a moral element in people's relation to work; people are 'good' if they work willingly to meet their responsibilities and 'bad' if they do not. Put together, these two notions suggest that the sample consider it a duty to make the most of one's natural ability:

> In order to be respectable and respected, people are expected to work hard and to be seen to be working hard to make the most of themselves and their natural advantages, or to put it another way, to overcome their natural disadvantages. (ibid., p. 70)

In addition to providing a moral framework by which to understand work itself, the 'public' accounts offer largely stereotypical images of what different types of work are like. These contrast with 'private' accounts that relate detailed personal feelings about what it is like to do a particular job.

Work in the home was differentiated on gender lines and this was justified by reproductive roles. Though there were some generational differences, this image was portrayed in 'public accounts'; of men and women fulfilling their rightful role within the family for the good of the family. 'Private' accounts were less predictable and concentrated more on individual personalities than general traits. It was in 'private' accounts, for example, that problems such as meanness with money or unkind child-care practises came to light. However, the function of 'private' accounts was not solely critical; they were related in a way that provided an opportunity for men and women to laugh at stressful aspects of their situation.

Again these data question Young and Willmott's analysis on both methodological and theoretical grounds. The research methods they used, suggests Cornwell, only gave them access to 'public' accounts of family life, precluding the more telling 'private' accounts. Young and Willmott's analyses rest heavily on their interpretation of women's strong relationships with their mothers being rooted in shared biological and emotional experiences of being a mother. In agreement with Young and Wilmott, Cornwell suggests that there is a reciprocal exchange of services between mothers and their married daughters:

> And having her so close as well, downstairs, she used to do all the washing as well. I used to take all me washing to her . . . she did, she used to do all the washing and all the ironing as well.   (ibid., p.90)

Whereas Young and Wilmott suggested that the closeness between mothers and their married daughters excluded men, Cornwell suggests that this was not the case because visits between women took place when men were working. Whether this indicates any real difference between Cornwell and Young and Wilmott is questionable because daughters still visited mothers without their husbands being present even if they were not at work.

(iii) *Health and illness*

The concepts of 'health' and 'illness' proved problematic for Cornwell early in the fieldwork stage of the research. Once some of the sample realized that they would be expected to talk about their health they wanted to drop out of the project because they argued that they and their families enjoyed good health. Some tried to direct Cornwell to other members of the community who were elderly and in poor health. Cornwell explained that the study was about 'health and illness in "ordinary people"' and that the sample would not be 'presented as people with particularly acute health problems' (ibid., p.124). This suggests that the sample saw good health as normal and illness as abnormal.

In 'public' accounts health and illness were portrayed as 'morally problematic' in much the same way as employment and unemployment. As with unemployment illness prevents people from meeting their responsibilities; it incapacitates and prevents people from working. Therefore, good health is perceived as a more morally acceptable condition than illness. Central to this is the question of 'otherness', which means that the individual was not responsible for the medical condition that prevented them from doing their paid work. An accident, for example, might precipitate a health problem where 'otherness' is not doubted. Generally it seems that 'good' people work hard and do not give in to poor health while 'bad' people take time away from work rather than stoically accepting the symptoms of poor health. Such people are often considered to be hypochondriacs who waste limited medical resources.

In contrast, 'private' accounts of illness take a less general view and concentrate on detailing the way that actual periods of illness affected interviewee's lives. Gender divisions became apparent when men expressed a kind of bravado at facing the risk of accidents at work and saw working through symptoms of ill-health as being masculine. At the same time men saw no contradiction in 'giving in' to symptoms when they were at home and being cared for by their wives so that they would be fit to work through the symptoms again the next day. It was expected that women would be the carers of family health despite their showing obvious resentment of additional domestic duties.

When women were ill they were more likely to visit the doctor, but this was not viewed as giving in to the condition. It was rather a matter of accommodating the illness; of expecting the doctor to provide something that would restore them to health quickly in order that they could get back to meeting their responsibilities. Moreover, the study indicated the extent to which women saw much ill-health as almost inevitable and, though related to lifestyle through child-bearing and poverty, beyond both their immediate control and that of the medical profession. Relationships with medical professionals were also the subject of differing 'public' and 'private' accounts. 'Public' accounts were elicited in answer to direct questions about interviewee's take-up of health care services and were generally 'admiring and respectful' of highly trained personnel. 'Private' accounts were more complex and often contradictory, relating experiences when the interviewee was dissatisfied with the medical care received. These accounts were personalised and consisted of criticisms of one particular hospital, doctor or nurse.

Critical Observations

The author suggests that her book is primarily an account of the perceptions of health and illness of a group of people in Bethnal Green. However, other scholars have shown most interest in Cornwell's distinction between 'public' and 'private' accounts, a contrast applauded as valuable by some and criticised as naive by others. Chandler (1991, p. 57), for example, acknowledges the distinction when she discusses how questions about the family sometimes lead interviewees to 'normalise' family life. Finch (1989, p. 79) also accepts Cornwell's reasoning when referring to the ways that public accounts of private relationships might obscure issues that might reflect badly on people being interviewed. A more negative view is presented by Frankenburg (1986) who, although he acknowledges the value of her empirical work and her findings, disputes the separation of 'public' and 'private' accounts. He argues that people frequently divulge very private and personal things about themselves and their families to complete strangers, with other passengers on train journeys, for example. Further, he suggests that what is said in private has much to do with conventions of what is right and proper behaviour and that 'private' and 'public' accounts are equally valid and 'real' but serve different purposes.

Frankenberg uses these points to argue that Cornwell's critique of Young and Willmott's (1957) community study of the same area is ill-founded firstly, because she was wrong in asserting that the study had been based totally on 'public' accounts and secondly, because Young and Willmott had not been trying to understand social meanings but had set out to document and analyse social processes. At worst, Frankenburg argues, Young and Willmott could be accused of misunderstanding public social processes.

Finch and Mason find the 'public'/'private' distinction sometimes helpful but argue that it can be 'potentially misleading, in that it implies that people have two fixed views of the world, one for public and one for private consumption' (1991, p. 365).

Lock (1986, p. 595), on the other hand, values the distinction suggesting that it helps us to understand how 'public' accounts are informed by medical knowledge, while the knowledge fails to be integrated into personal health-care provision (for example, knowledge of the link between tobacco and cancer amongst smokers), and why general health promotion schemes are unlikely to have the desired impact.

Conclusion

Hard-Earned Lives provides a more coherent examination of the perception of lay people to matters of health, illness and medical service provision than is usual. In this account a clear and systematic distinction is made between 'public' and 'private' types of account, the ways in which they were collected, and the implications of them for health service provision and for future ethnographers. The study indicates, for example, that much-needed preventive medicine and community services are undervalued, stemming from lay people accepting uncritically many ideas and values current in the dominant medical profession. For ethnographers, if accepted, the 'public'/'private' distinction clarifies the status accorded to data and highlights the 'expert' status often given to researchers by interviewees.

Bibliography and Further Reading

Bell, C. and Newby, H. (1972), *Community Studies. An Introduction to the Sociology of the Local Community*, London, Allen and Unwin.
Chandler, J. (1991), *Women without Husbands: An Exploration of the Margins of Marriage*, London, Macmillan Education.
Cornwell, J. (1984), *Hard-Earned Lives*, London, Tavistock.

Finch, J. (1989), *Family Obligation and Social Change*, Cambridge, Polity Press.

Finch, J. and Mason, J. (1991), 'Obligations of Kinship in Contemporary Britain – Is There Normative Agreement?' in *British Journal of Sociology*, Vol. 42, No. 3, pp. 354–367.

Frankenberg, R. (1986), Review of 'Hard-Earned Lives' in *Sociology of Health and Illness*, Vol. 8, No.1, pp. 99–100.

Lock, M. (1986), Review of 'Hard-Earned Lives' in *American Ethnologist*, Vol. 13, No. 3, pp. 594–595.

Marris, P. (1974), *Loss and Change*, London, Routledge and Kegan Paul.

Young, M. and Willmott, P. (1959), *Family and Kinship in East London*, London, Routledge and Kegan Paul.

Acknowledgements

The authors and publishers would like to thank the following for permission to reproduce copyright material:

Central Statistical Office for the tables from *Social Trends, 1993*; Macmillan Press Ltd. and Jan Pahl for the tables and figure from *Money and Marriage*; Tavistock and Sandra Wallman for the two figures from *Eight London Households*; Routledge and Janet Finch and Jennifer Mason for the table and example from *Negotiating Family Responsibilities*; Professor Valerie Walkerdine for the table from her and Helen Lucey's *Democracy in the Kitchen*; Dr Nickie Charles and Marion Kerr for the table from *Women, Food and Families*; Routledge and Jane Wheelock for the table from *Husbands at Home*; Comedia and David Morley for the table from *Family Television: Cultural Power and Domestic Leisure*; Routledge and Patricia Allatt and Susan Yeandle for the tables from *Youth Unemployment and the Family: Voices of Disordered Times*; Blackwell and Dr Annette Lawson for the table from *Adultery: An Analysis of Love and Betrayal*; Blackwell and Liz Kelly for the tables from *Surviving Sexual Violence*; Avebury and Jane Millar for the tables from *Poverty and the Lone-parent Family: the challenge of social policy*.

Every effort has been made to obtain permissions but the publishers would be pleased to hear from any unacknowledged source and full acknowledgement will be made at the first opportunity.